MEANT TO BE SHARED

True Stories of God's Presence in the Life of an Ordinary Person

Kimberly Shaw

MEANT TO BE SHARED:

True Stories of God's Presence in the Life of an Ordinary Person.

This Book Belongs to:

Dedicated to those searching for the way to truth and life.

"Ask, and it will be given to you; seek, and you will find;
knock, and it will be opened to you.
For everyone who asks receives, and he who seeks finds,
and to him who knocks it will be opened."
Matthew 7:7-8

CONTENTS

PSALM 23 (NLT)

"The LORD is my shepherd;
　　I have all that I need.
He lets me rest in green meadows;
　　he leads me beside peaceful streams.
　　He renews my strength.
He guides me along right paths,
　　bringing honor to his name.
Even when I walk
　　through the darkest valley,
I will not be afraid,
　　for you are close beside me.
Your rod and your staff
　　protect and comfort me.
You prepare a feast for me
　　in the presence of my enemies.
You honor me by anointing my head with oil.
　　My cup overflows with blessings.
Surely your goodness and unfailing love will pursue me
　　all the days of my life,
and I will live in the house of the LORD forever."

God uses ordinary things like donuts, frogs, and surfboards to prove He is ever present. He uses ordinary events such as going to the market, commuting to work, or trimming a tree to reveal He is orchestrating every detail of our lives. But He is far from ordinary. For even in the midst of struggle God proves His redemptive power over our circumstances. God is amazing, powerful, surprising, loving, caring and in control.

The writing of this book began on my fifty-fifth birthday. It was a Sunday morning. I was suddenly woken by an impressionable thought that spoke to my heart and mind. The thought, not my own, said, "Your God stories are not yours, they are Mine, and they are meant to be shared." I knew it was God speaking to me.

If you are wondering what God's voice sounds like, I hope these stories will reveal that to you. If you doubt God is active in people's lives, I pray these stories will convince you otherwise. Then I hope you will begin to discover His presence in your own life.

But I confess; many times I doubted God's leadings, especially when I didn't understand His message. But even in my doubting, God continued to teach me to hear and trust Him. I learned to discern God's voice from an unexplainable sensation of knowing I should act on a thought or word or feeling.

God doesn't typically shout at us in a loud audible voice, though I'm not suggesting He never has nor will do. As told in the fifth story, "Collision with Truth," God used lightning to get someone's attention. But it's been my observation that when He speaks to us personally He speaks in a still, small voice. Like a whisper, it causes us to be still, to draw close to Him, and pay special attention. The story in 1Kings 19:11-13, illustrates this. The story starts with God *talking* to Elijah.

> "*Then He said, 'Go out, and stand on the mountain before the LORD' And behold, the LORD passed by, and a great and strong wind tore into the mountains and broke the rocks in pieces before the LORD, but the LORD was not in the wind; and after the wind an earthquake, but the LORD was not in the earthquake; and after the earthquake a fire, but the LORD was not in the fire; and after the fire **a still, small voice**. So it was, when Elijah heard it, that he wrapped his face in his mantle and went out and stood in the entrance of the cave. Suddenly a **voice** came to him, and said, 'What are you doing here, Elijah?'*" (Emphasis mine)

This is the character of God I have come to know. He doesn't typically communicate through the destructive force of wind, or an earthquake, or fire. When speaking to us personally, God converses in a non-threatening still small voice so as to not frighten us. He cares for us and loves us deeply. He desires us to know Him and love Him in return.

These stories are written in chronological order, yet each story stands on its own. Reading them in order demonstrates how God used early events to increase my faith in circumstances that followed. If the early stories sound like they are about an immature person, they are. I was in my early 20s when I first came to know Jesus as my personal Lord and Savior. If some stories sound like I struggled to comprehend what God was saying, it's because I did struggle. It wasn't until after I acted on faith of what I believed to be God's voice, He then confirmed it by the outcome of the circumstances. The outcome was always a blessing.

If you are seeking stories on specific topics, a list in the back of the book groups stories in categories. God often repeated the way He revealed Himself, while at other times He was completely surprising. Topics include protection, provision, guidance, healing, answered prayer, angels, and small miracles.

The names of others in these stories were intentionally omitted in an effort to magnify what God was doing in each circumstance. Where the story is clearer by using the person's name, it was included.

There is nothing special about me. I am only an ordinary person. The only One who is truly amazing is the Almighty God, His Son and Savior Jesus, and the Holy Spirit who comforts and guides us. He is the One I wish to point you to. He is the only One who can do the miraculous. I trust He will use these stories to draw you closer to Him, to prove His great power, and reveal His deep love for you.

If at any time you need validation that I'm an ordinary person, read my story titled "Paper" in the back of the book. If God is willing to interact with a silly dork like me, He is willing to participate in the life of everyone. By picking up this book, I believe He has already begun conversing with you.

I can't predict what God intends to do with these stories. I know He's going to use them; otherwise He wouldn't have been so persistent in getting me to share them. Nor would He allow me to experience Him in these events in the first place. A part of me struggled with publishing this book. Sharing some of these personal stories means I had to be vulnerable. Yet God constantly reminded me that when I gave my life to Him I also became His vessel to be used for His purposes. These stories aren't about me; they are about Him. They are His stories, and they are meant to be shared.

FAITHFUL WITNESSES
Family speaks of God

The first God stories I heard were stories that began with hardship and tragedy. As a young girl, I heard these stories while lingering at the dining table with older family members. I was probably enjoying a second helping of dessert. Someone would say, "Remember when Grandma and Grandpa almost lost the farm?" Someone else would reply, "Grandma was sick with worry, praying hard." Followed by the response, "It was a miracle God provided the money in the eleventh hour." Another added, "The last minute of the eleventh hour!" Through the retelling of their stories, the evidence of a God who comforts and saves those who cry out to Him became apparent. Here are two of those stories I grew up hearing.

Maria is my paternal great-grandmother. Through her, I learned God answers prayer. It was her farm God miraculously saved. On another occasion, she thought she lost her husband. It was in the early days of the automobile. My great-grandfather and his cousin drove their open touring car to a town thirty-five miles away. This was a long distance when roads were rough and often unmarked. They anticipated returning home by sundown, but when evening came they had not returned.

After the children were asleep, my great-grandmother, threw herself on her bed and began to pray for the safety of the two men. Through the window of her upstairs bedroom two men stepped into her room wearing brilliant white, surrounded by a radiant light. She believed they were angels. They spoke to her in German, "Rest in peace, the men are safe under my sheltering wings." Without turning around, the angels disappeared into the evening sky.

My great-grandmother fell into a deep sleep. The next morning, she was able to confidently reassure her children that their father and uncle would return home safe. Before sundown, both men arrived unharmed.

Katherine is my maternal grandmother. When she was ten years old her father was badly injured. While hunting in the woods, he stopped to rest. Napping beside a tree his gun fell from where he propped it up, causing it to fire and shoot him. He was able to get hold of his horse that dragged him home.

While Katherine sat at his bedside he drifted into eternity. As he did, he described to her what he saw in heaven. I never learned what he said about heaven, but its description explains why my grandmother had such a desire to share Jesus with others.

In the midst of this tragic story God comforted and encouraged a little girl who was losing her father. Because of her father's faith, he was given a view of heaven that gave her an eternal hope that influenced her faith in God for the rest of her life. As a result, my grandmother became instrumental in my faith.

It's my prayer the following stories will cause you to recognize the miraculous acts of God in your life. Then I encourage you to share your God stories with your family. Your stories validate the existence of God, prove He is active in people's lives, and increase the faith of others.

In case you're thinking, "I don't have any God stories," keep reading. I'm sure you do but just haven't noticed them. For example, have you ever had an intuition to do, or not do, something and realize later it was a helpful instruction or blessing? I believe this is the Holy Spirit guiding us. Have you seen a need miraculously met? God's presence isn't only in the struggle, but in every detail of our lives.

"Return to your own house, and tell what great things God has done for you." And he went his way and proclaimed throughout the whole city what great things Jesus had done for him.
Luke 8:39

DONUTS WITH GRANDMA

God seen in others

My maternal grandmother laid the foundation for my belief in God. It wasn't what she taught me about Jesus that solidified my faith, but how she lived her life.

When I was a child I occasionally stayed at her house for the weekend. On Sunday morning before going to church, she took me to the donut shop. It was a long, narrow shop with a glass display of assorted donuts on one side. On the other side, we encountered homeless-looking men each sitting at their own table.

While I eyed the donuts, Grandma greeted each man. She told them that God loved them, and then ask if she could give them a ride to church. I can still see her in my mind's eye pointing down the street out the tall front windows in the direction of church.

At first, her actions shocked me. Grandma was an elegant woman. She was always dressed well, her hair was always styled, and her perfectly applied makeup brought out the cheerfulness in her face. Her home was a dreamy cottage, and her car, a turquoise Thunderbird, was equally impeccable.

It was inconceivable at my age that she would let an unwashed stranger in her car with us. Later I discovered she told others about Jesus in the presence of all her grandchildren. While I thought I was about to receive the blessing of a donut, she was actually blessing me with eternal things. She was showing me how to love others and how to share the good news of God's salvation to everyone. Jesus, through her, greeted each stranger and offered him hope in the way of an invitation.

My grandmother's acts have forever encouraged me to grab every opportunity to share God with those I come in contact with. Her small interactions with others actually became life changing for me. So, I encourage you, if you are a believer, make the most of every opportunity to tell others about God. It will not only be life changing for them, but for all those in your sphere of influence.

And He said to them,
"Go into all the world and
preach the gospel to every creature."
Mark 16:15

SHOP WOMAN

God speaks through others

This was one of those days when everything seemed to go wrong. I already had a rough day at college. On the way home from school my car broke down on a busy road lined with shops. I left my car parked on the side of the road, grabbed my heavy overstuffed art bag, and started walking home. This was before cell phones. I wasn't looking forward to the walk home, mainly because of the very steep hill leading up to the house.

To make matters worse, my next-door neighbor drove past me on her way home. She honked, threw her arm out the window, waved, and shouted a hearty greeting as she sped by. I was disheartened. The afternoon was hot, and the weight of my huge school bag dug into my shoulder.

When I turned the corner, a woman came out from one of the shops and heartedly said to me with a smile, "Jesus loves you!"

Her boldness startled me. As a child, I often went to church and sang, "Jesus loves me this I know, for the Bible tells me so." But it had been a long time since I attended church. I wondered what compelled her to run out onto the sidewalk to tell a stranger this good news. She had no way of knowing the terrible day I had. But God knew and used her to convey His encouraging message.

The Bible says that Jesus is the Creator of everything. Everything extends past the physical world we see around us. He is also the Creator of every era, event, and circumstance. For example, if my car did not break down, or if my neighbor gave me a ride home, I would have missed God's message.

Looking back, I'm glad for the troubles I had that day. This woman taught me something that no one else could at the time. She reminded me of the truth that God loved me. She also showed me what a person yielded to the Holy Spirit looks like.

When your day seems out of whack, ask yourself, "Is it really?" Try to slow down and listen to what God is trying to say to you. When you feel a tug to do something that doesn't make sense, like tell a stranger Jesus loves them, are you willing to do it? It was this simple act that began the ultimate call on my life to follow Jesus.

"...and for me, that utterance may be given to me,
that I may open my mouth boldly to make known
the mystery of the gospel,"
Ephesians 6:19

THE COMMUTE
God leads us to Himself

God was persistent. He didn't give up on me even though I was unresponsive and stubborn. It took an accident to finally get my attention. This is my personal story of how I came to know Jesus as my Lord and Savior.

As a child, I went to church with my family. I heard many Bible stories in Sunday school and had no doubt God existed. In my early teens, my family stopped going to church, choosing instead to go camping on weekends. In the summer, we water-skied. In winter, we hauled motorcycles to off-road destinations.

Invitations to make a decision to follow Christ came when I started working in Los Angeles. To get to work I avoided the freeway traffic by taking a commuter bus into downtown from where I lived an hour away. At my bus stop in L.A., church groups handed out gospel tracts to those of us exiting the bus. I never read them, but I couldn't throw them away either. The people reminded me of my grandmother and I knew what they were sharing contained truth. I put the tiny pamphlets in my purse until a thick layer lined the bottom of it.

Next, a co-worker told me about Jesus. I didn't take this co-worker's word seriously. Before he became a Christian, he was, in my opinion, a womanizer. I saw him being affectionate with three girls in one day. To me this appeared disrespectful to two of them, so my impression of him was already low. I had a hard time listening to what he said about Jesus even though he became a completely different person after giving his life to Christ. His whole countenance had changed into one full of an obvious joy. It was so noticeable that the entire office staff was asking each other what they thought happened to him. In his zeal for the Lord, he told me about Jesus often, trying to convince me to also accept Him as my Savior.

When I didn't heed the handouts at the bus stop, and refused to listen to my co-worker, God set in motion a third invitation. It began on a crowded bus commuting home from work. An obnoxious group of friends sat together in the back of the bus. When they weren't telling dirty jokes, they played cards on their briefcases, loudly shouting at every win or loss. I avoided them.

On this particular ride home, the only seat I found was in the back of the bus next to the most obnoxious old man. I grudgingly sat down and tried to ignore him. He pursued a conversation with me by telling crude jokes. When I didn't respond to him he said, "See that young man up there reading his Bible? You should sit next to him and try to corrupt him."

I changed seats immediately. I was mainly relieved to know there was another seat available. I was also curious to know what he was reading in the Bible.

I greeted him and asked him his name. He replied, "Timothy." I asked him what he was reading in the Bible. He answered, "The book of Timothy." I found this highly coincidental. I asked him why he was reading the Bible, to which he said, "I want to learn more about God."

Seeing someone reading the Bible on their own simply to learn about God was impressive. I couldn't remember seeing anyone in my family doing that. Whenever I saw him on the bus I sat next to him. I had become more willing to know about God. He kindly answered all my questions over the weeks that followed.

Not long after this, I got a new car. It wasn't brand new, but it was new to me, a 1980 Buick Regal. Tired of waiting for the bus, I decided to drive into downtown instead. I offered those on the bus to ride with me in exchange for help with gas, which would cost less than the monthly bus fare. My new carpool buddies were Timothy, an older woman I recently met, and the obnoxious old man I sat next to in the back of the bus. I can't remember how he was invited.

Commuting together abruptly ended when we were involved in a terrible accident on the freeway. My car was rear-ended and pushed into the car in front of me. I suffered a double whiplash. The old man and woman sitting in the back seat were also injured. Timothy, the only Christian in the car, remained unharmed. It appeared as though God had protected him, and I wondered if God was able to keep His followers safe.

I was taken to the hospital. While waiting alone in the patient's room, a strange thought continually repeated in my mind, "Ecclesiastes, Ecclesiastes, Ecclesiastes." I couldn't make it go away. I knew it was a book in the Bible, but I had no idea what it said. When I got home I opened the children's Bible my grandmother gave me. Ecclesiastes Chapter 3:2-8 caught my attention and I began to read it.

"To everything there is a season,
A time for every purpose under heaven:
A time to be born, and a time to die;
A time to plant, and a time to pluck what is planted;
A time to kill, and a time to heal;
A time to break down, and a time to build up;
A time to weep, and a time to laugh;
A time to mourn, and a time to dance;
A time to cast away stones, and a time to gather stones;
A time to embrace, and a time to refrain from embracing;
A time to gain, and a time to lose;
A time to keep, and a time to throw away;
A time to tear, and a time to sew;
A time to keep silence, and a time to speak;
A time to love, and a time to hate;
A time of war, and a time of peace."

I started to cry seeing the pattern of contrasting circumstances. My life felt broken down and filled with sorrow. I had no joy and my heart ached for it. I wondered if God could create something good in my life. I responded with, "God, if you are real, then prove it to me." I thought if there really was a living God then He was capable of proving His existence to me.

I spent the following weeks in physical therapy. When I returned to work my co-worker, who told me about Jesus, was there to encourage me. He invited me to a movie that would play at a church near my home on the following Friday. After my recent experiences, I was finally willing to go. Since my car was still in the repair shop, my co-worker offered to drive me to the church and take me home afterward. This was an extremely generous offer since he lived on the other side of Los Angeles. I accepted his invitation. I was searching for answers.

The movie shown at church was, "A Thief in the Night." It was a drama about the end times rapture and the beginning of the great tribulation. The story emphasized Matthew 24:40-41,44:

"Then two men will be in the field: one will be taken and the other left. Two women will be grinding at the mill: one will be taken and the other left. Therefore, you also be ready, for the Son of Man is coming at an hour you do not expect."

At the end of the movie, an invitation was offered to give one's life to Jesus and accept Him as Savior. I sensed a powerful tug on my heart and was moved to tears. I knew I was lost without Jesus. I knew He was calling me to Himself. Unable to resist, I went forward and gave my life to Christ.

Afterward, my co-worker confessed his struggle of trying to lead me to Christ. He said in his initial zeal as a new believer he was determined to save me. He became frustrated when I didn't respond. He told God, "I can't save her, God. She might just as well go to hell."

To which God responded, "You're right. You can't save her, only I can. I'm the only One who saves."

My dad called the following morning after I accepted Jesus as my Savior. My parents lived 500 miles away. He said, "We believe something happened to you last night. Did anything happen?" My parents were already believers.

"Yes, Dad, I gave my life to Jesus. I'm saved. I'm a Christian." He said he and my mom thought so and had to call to see if what they felt was true.

When I share the good news of Jesus with others and they question if what I'm saying is true, I encourage them to ask God to prove to them He is real. For if there is a God, then He is real. If God is real, then He is powerful enough to prove He is God.

The following stories demonstrate God's existence in my personal life, where He has perpetually proven Himself to me. In each instance He also revealed a new attribute about Himself. If He has done this for me, I know He can prove Himself to you as well.

Jesus says,
"Behold, I stand at the door and knock.
If anyone hears my voice and opens the door,
I will come in to him and dine with him, and he with Me."
Revelation 3:20

And,
"For God so loved the world that he gave his only begotten Son,
that whoever believes in him should not perish
but have everlasting life."
John 3:16

COLLISION WITH TRUTH
God restores lives

Remember the Buick in my last story that was rear-ended on the freeway in rush hour traffic? God still had plans for her. The car was deemed a total wreck, yet it was cheaper to repair it than replace it. It was towed to a recommended shop in West Los Angeles that was closer to work than home. When the repairs were completed, the shop owner called to say he was sending one of his employees in my car to pick me up at work. From there I would drive the employee back to the shop.

I need to clarify what I'm about to say next because it's NOT my current belief. At the time, I had a false prejudice that led to an inappropriate fear of others. When I was a young girl it was stressed that I should not get in the car with strangers. An appropriate teaching to keep children safe, but this instruction was emphasized by naming specific ethic groups. As you read the following paragraphs don't jump to conclusions too quickly. I need to first be honest about my misguided assumption to reveal how God used this event to dispel that false sense of fear.

I waited outside on the sidewalk in front of my office building for my car to arrive. I was thrilled when I saw it pull up looking as good as new. My enthusiasm soon turned to agitation when the employee who was sent to fetch me stepped out of the driver seat. He was a tall lean black guy, a little older than me, with a large Afro. With childhood warnings running through my mind, I suddenly became fearful.

I was afraid to get in the car with him, but I didn't have another option. With a big smile, he politely held the driver's door open for me to get in, then quickly ran around to the passenger side. He gave me directions to the shop as I remained quiet. Inside I was fuming as my fear turned to anger. My misguided thoughts mimicked those I heard as a child. I remember wondering who thought it was a good idea to send this guy to pick up a white girl in downtown Los Angeles? Horrific thought, right? I warned you it was bad. But please don't throw the book aside just yet or you'll miss the mighty act of God that dispelled my unrealistic fear.

As I drove, my passenger broke the silence to tell me his story. He said, "You know that bumper sticker you had on your car, the one that read, "I LOVE JESUS"? I had to look at that every day for six weeks while I put your car back together. Each time I saw it I was reminded of the stories my mama told me about Jesus when I was a boy. I remembered her telling me that Jesus sees everything I do and knows everywhere I go. If I'm doing something I'm not supposed to be doing, or if I'm somewhere I'm not supposed to be, Jesus can make lightning strike. Well, that's what happened. When I was a boy I was somewhere I wasn't supposed to be, doing something I wasn't supposed to be doing. Right then, right there, a bolt of lightning hit the porch where I was standing. While working on your car I was thinking about my life, how I'm not living as I should be. So, with all this work I've been doing on your car, I've had a lot of time to think, and I want to tell you, I rededicated my life to Jesus. I'm living for Him again."

What do you think happened to my fear, agitation, and ignorance? God removed them and inserted His marvelous love for this young man. By God's incredible handiwork He used a wrecked car to lead a young man back to Him. Then God used that redeemed young man to repair the messed-up notions that dwelt inside of my own heart.

"For My thoughts are not your thoughts,
nor are your ways My ways," says the LORD.
"For as the heavens are higher than the earth,
So are My ways higher than your ways,
And My thoughts than your thoughts."
Isaiah 55:8-9

CONTACT LENS
Nothing is too small for God

In my 20s I wore contact lenses. One morning, while getting ready for work, I had trouble applying one contact lens. It folded, lodged in the corner of my eye, and then it wouldn't remain on my eye. Instead it stayed stuck to the tip of my finger. It took so long to finish this simple task that I worried about being late for work. Frustrated I yelled out, "God, this is ridiculous! Please help me!"

With the lens a half inch away from my eye, it suddenly popped off my finger, flew through the air, and landed dead center on my eye. I was astonished, especially considering my bad attitude in which I spoke to God.

This may not seem like a significant God story worth mentioning. But like this story, I often struggle doing tasks without asking God for help. Throughout my life God brought this event to mind. Each time He used it to remind me that He is willing to help with every struggle no matter how insignificant the need is. It's funny to think it took the difficulty of putting in a contact lens to help me *see* this.

"Ask, and it will be given to you;
seek, and you will find;
knock, and it will be opened to you."
Matthew 7:7

GIFT IN SECRET
God's Word guides us

My boss was in a foul mood all morning. I never saw him like this before. He was typically even-tempered, happy most of the time. It wasn't clear what he was angry about. He already yelled at several people who walked into his office. You could tell they weren't prepared for it. Some of them simply turned around and walked out confused. I avoided him by staying at my desk safely hidden behind my cubicle wall.

When it was time to go to lunch I walked to my favorite café where I also read my Bible. I was previously reading Proverbs, so I continued where I left off. In chapter 21, verse 14, I read,

"A gift given in secret subdues anger."

I wondered if secretly giving my boss a gift would really subdue his anger. Wanting to test this verse, I left the café early and walked to the nearest convenience store seeking something to give him. Only one thing caught my attention, a roll of rainbow

LifeSavers on a narrow shelf opposite the cash register. They seemed like such an insignificant gift. I couldn't imagine how they would subdue the anger I saw that morning. However, something kept drawing my attention back to them that I couldn't resist.

I bought the LifeSavers and quickly went back to work to sneak them in his office. I placed them on his desk in front of his chair, then returned to my desk and waited.

When my boss entered his office he yelled out, but this time in a joyful tone, "Who put these LifeSavers on my desk? Who knew these were my favorite!"

Of course, I had no way of knowing Lifesavers were his favorite, but God did. I then knew why the LifeSavers made such an impression on me in the store. The Holy Spirit knew they were the perfect gift and directed me to them.

My boss asked everyone that passed his office if they gave him the LifeSavers. Most of them just nodded they hadn't as if they were avoiding getting yelled at again. He never asked me, and I wasn't going to tell him, it was meant to be a secret. Of course, it isn't anymore, but at the time, that colorful candy cheered him up. He was like a little kid trying to figure out who gave him his favorite candy.

I learned the Bible has an answer for every issue, even an angry boss. I also learned to trust the leading of the Holy Spirit even if it didn't make sense. In this circumstance, God's Word proved to be truly LifeSaving! (pun intended)

"For the word of God is living and powerful, and sharper than any two-edged sword, piercing even to the division of soul and spirit, and of joints and marrow, and is a discerner of the thoughts and intents of the heart."
Hebrews 4:12

CITY OF ANGELS
God's Angels protect us

An unexpected meeting occurred when I was in my mid-20s working in Los Angeles. My morning began with an early bus commute into downtown to avoid the rush hour traffic. I went to Clifton's Cafeteria on Broadway near 7th Street. There I enjoyed a leisurely breakfast while reading my Bible before going to work.

This particular morning it had been raining. The old sidewalks in that part of Los Angeles were inlaid with designs of polished stone, such as marble or granite. When it rained they became slippery. That day I was wearing flat shoes with smooth soles.

When I finished breakfast, I left the cafeteria to walk the seven blocks to the office where I worked. I was careful to take small purposeful steps to avoid slipping. An uneasy feeling came over me and I noticed I was the only one on the sidewalk for the entire block on both sides. This was odd because it was rush hour when people were racing to work. There also weren't any cars on the road. I was nervous because young women shouldn't walk the streets of downtown L.A. alone.

Moments later three guys rounded the corner in front of me. They walked towards me, shoulder to shoulder, taking up most of the width of the sidewalk. From their dress and manner in which they walked, they appeared to be gang members. I wasn't being judgmental, only realistic, trying to stay safe. News of gangs killing others in L.A. was normal. Now it looked like three were on the same sidewalk walking towards me. No businesses were open for me to take refuge in, and Clifton's was too far away to return to. I was afraid.

Instantly a true story I previously read came to mind of angels who protected a missionary family. Men from a nearby village surrounded the missionary's house in order to attack them. The attackers never approached the house because they saw soldiers on the roof. The missionaries later learned what the attackers saw and believed the soldiers to be angels, as they had no knowledge of anyone on their roof. Remembering this story, I quickly prayed, "Lord, I need two gigantic angels right now, one on each side of me. I don't need to see them, but the three guys walking towards me do."

After I prayed I simply put my trust in God. I'm not sure why I asked for two angels. There were three guys walking towards me, and the story I remembered had an army of angels. In my mind I believed if they were large enough they could keep me safe.

The moment the three guys were in front of me, my flat slick shoe suddenly slipped on the smooth sidewalk. I started to fall. I remember thinking, "I'm a goner. Once I'm on the ground, I'm an easy target." But that's not what happened. I never hit the ground.

The three guys reached out for me, but instead of attacking me, they grabbed me under my arms and lifted me up to my feet. One of them asked in a sweet tone of voice unlike that of a thug, "Are you alright?" It all seemed so unreal: a saved catch, a helping hand, and a kind question from three unlikely guys.

Stunned, I had mixed feelings of shock, relief, and embarrassment from slipping. Once back on my way to work, and the three others now behind me, I prayed again. This time I ask God, "What was that? What just happened?"

A peaceful thought flooded my heart and mind with, "Those were your angels. They are the ones I sent in answer to your prayer. There were other dangers you couldn't see."

I asked God for two angels. He sent three.

I hope this story is a source of great comfort to you. God provides exactly what we need even before we ask, and often in a different way than we expect it. He is always teaching His followers something about Himself: His power, His protection, His love and faithfulness to those who seek to know Him more.

"For He shall give His angels charge over you,
to keep you in all your ways.
In their hands they shall bear you up,
lest you dash your foot against a stone."
Psalm 91:11-12

PICK HER UP!

Learning to hear God's voice

It was dark as I left the church parking lot after Wednesday night Bible study. I stopped at the driveway waiting to turn right when traffic cleared. To my left a woman was sitting on the bus stop bench in front of a small building on the corner. A thought entered my mind that said, "Pick her up."

I ignored the thought, turned right, and drove towards home. I wasn't convinced what I heard was from God. I thought the idea came from my own concern for her of having to wait for a ride in the dark. My own reasoning convinced me it wasn't safe to offer a ride to a stranger. Besides, I only had enough gas in my car to get home. I also didn't have any money to buy more gas.

Payday was the next morning by automatic bank deposit. Driving the woman to where she needed to go encroached on my precalculated plans. I only had enough gas to drive to church, back home, to the ATM in the morning, and then to the gas station. I pre-calculated the amount of fuel in the car, its miles per gallon, and the driving distance round trip before deciding if I could drive to church that evening. I could not believe God would ask me to give someone a ride if it meant I would be stranded on my way home.

Yet, the request was repeated, "Pick her up." I ignored it again and continued driving away from her. My heart began to pound, a little at first, then harder, and then harder still. The request intensified until it was more like a demand.

"Pick her up!" "Pick her up!!" "Pick her up!!!"

I could no longer ignore God. Out loud I shouted back in rebuttal, "OK! But You better make the gas in my car last!" I was thinking of the Israelites who walked through the wilderness for forty years without their shoes wearing out. If God could make shoes last for forty years, I imagined He could also make gas last longer in a car.

I turned around, but I still needed more assurance. I was resistant to obey, mainly because I was afraid. She was still sitting on the bench. I drove into the parking lot and parked behind the small building on the corner to block her view of me. Before I offered her a ride I asked God for a specific Bible verse that would confirm I was hearing Him correctly.

A thought entered my mind, "Read Hebrews 13." I turned to the chapter to find written in the first two verses,

"Let brotherly love continue. Do not forget to entertain strangers, for by doing so some have unwittingly entertained angels."

Enthusiasm replaced my doubt and fear. God could not have been clearer. The idea of having an angel in my car was exhilarating. I wondered what we would talk about. I hoped she would tell me more about God, about heaven, about angels.

I drove around the small building and rolled down my passenger window in anticipation of offering her a ride. But when I rounded the corner the bench was empty. I was sure I didn't see a bus. I know because I purposely positioned myself in the parking lot towards the oncoming traffic so as to see if a bus drove by. That way, if a bus did arrive, I would be off the hook for giving her a ride. But now I was truly disappointed.

Unconcerned with the low fuel level, I raced ahead to see if I could find a bus that I may have missed. I even drove farther down the street past my turn home, but I couldn't find a bus. When I decided to turn around and drive home, there was no evidence my fuel had decreased.

Looking back at this event, I can only conclude it was a test. God was teaching me to hear His voice. He was instructing me to obey Him. He was ultimately teaching me to trust Him.

The next time God asked me to offer someone a ride I was more willing to yield to His direction. That story, "Pull Over" follows this one. I was still hesitant, still afraid, and still in need of an answer from the Bible. God again made His instructions clear and confirmed it was Him speaking to me.

"My sheep hear My voice,
and I know them,
and they follow Me."
John 10:27

PULL OVER!

God teaches us to trust Him

Dear reader, this story comes with a warning. Please don't offer a stranger a ride, especially if you are a young lady, unless you are absolutely sure the Holy Spirit is leading you to do so. Move slowly, seek the Bible for answers, and listen intently for God's voice. Do not act on your own empathetic tendencies. This event began with God's instructions to pick up a woman at a bus stop several weeks earlier. That instruction was followed by a radio testimony of a similar occurrence.

The work is His, it's not ours. So again, I caution you, do not do this type of work in your own effort. Instead, be led by the Holy Spirit and you'll experience the unforgettable, powerful hand of God in people's lives.

It was a Friday night. I was on the freeway driving to church when a distinct thought flooded my heart and mind. It urgently said, "Pull over!"

Earlier that week I heard a similar testimony on the radio. A man heard the same thing spoken to him while he was driving on the highway. Believing the Holy Spirit was instructing him, he drove his car onto the shoulder. On the side of the road his tire went flat, saving him from a blowout at high speeds. He attributed it as God's protection.

With an off-ramp ahead of me, I slowed down and exited the freeway. As nothing happened to my car I continued driving slowly to church, taking the side streets the rest of the way.

I heard God's instruction again. This time it was more urgent than before. "Stop! Pull over!"

I pulled my car over, parked at the curb, and prayed, "Lord, reveal to me in your Word what you are saying."

Another thought came to mind, "Ezekiel 44." I turned the overhead dome light on, opened my Bible to the text, but it made no sense to me. I prayed again, this time I heard the thought slower, "Ezekiel 40:4." Turning to that verse I read,

> "...look with your eyes and hear with your ears,
> and fix your mind on everything I show you;
> for you were brought here so that I might show them to you.
> Declare to the house of Israel everything you see."

Previously I studied Christ's second coming, so I thought this must be it! Jesus is coming back now! I assumed God had me stop the car for the safety of others. That way when I was raptured out my car to go be with Him, my car wouldn't be out of control. I was so excited! I grabbed the top of my steering wheel, pulled myself forward, and intently looked up into the night sky anticipating His miraculous return. But as you know, that didn't happen.

I read the verse again and then turned off the dome light to look outside at my surroundings. I wondered what God was trying to show me. Across the street to the left was an old shopping center. There were a few dim exterior lights still on, though most of the shops looked closed. To the right was a block wall that separated the back yard of a home from the wide cement sidewalk. A tree from the back yard grew over the wall with its branches almost touching the ground. As my eyes adjusted to the dark I saw a metal shopping cart turned on its side within the branches of the tree. Behind the shopping cart was a young man sitting on the ground. He looked to be about my age in his early 20s.

I remember feeling embarrassed thinking he saw me in the car with the dome light on. I wandered what he thought when I clutched the top of the steering wheel, pulled myself forward, and looked up into the night sky. Then a thought, not my own, came to mind, "Ask him if he is a Christian."

A little fearful, I rolled the window down only two inches and shouted out over the top of it, "Are you a Christian?"

He yelled back, without getting up, "I used to be."

Another thought came to mind, "Tell him why you are here." I rolled the window down half way and described how I came to be parked exactly where he was sitting. I then asked him why he was there.

He answered, "I was just at the bar across the street until I got beat up. Before that I was kicked out of the house where I was living, so now I'm here under this tree. I have nowhere else to go."

It was obvious God led me to him for a reason. I rolled my window down the rest of the way and leaned over the passenger seat toward him. I explained how it wasn't a coincidence that God directed me to pull over and stop exactly where he was sitting. I told him I was on my way to church, and I believed God wanted him to go with me. I explain that on Friday night they usually showed a movie, or a band played. This was the same church my co-worker took me to where I gave my life to Christ. I thought God might be calling this guy to Himself, also.

He argued that everything he owned was in his backpack and he wasn't sure if it was safe to get in the car with me. Realizing he was more afraid of me than I was of him, I felt comfortable to continue persuading him to go to church. He finally relented and got in the car. The smell of alcohol was strong.

Because we arrived at church late, an usher directed us where to sit. Once we were seated, someone two rows behind stood up and called out to my passenger. It was a friend of his who excitedly shouted to him, "Dude, where have you been? You won't believe what's happened to me since we got kicked out of that house. Dude, I got saved. I can't believe you are here, I've been praying for you, man."

We were interrupted when the music stopped and the service began. When we sat down and faced forward, there wasn't a movie or a band. Instead, a man I had never seen before got up and began speaking. He started off by saying, "You may be here today completely drunk out of your mind and have no idea how you got here. But I'm here to tell you God loves you."

I was already overwhelmed by my passenger's friend sitting behind us. I became even more shocked by the speaker's opening statement that I barely heard anything else he said. At the end of the man's talk he gave an altar call, inviting people forward to accept Jesus as their personal Savior.

Again, my passenger's friend popped up out of his seat. He reached over the people sitting in the pew between us and tapped his friend on the shoulder saying, "That's for you, man! You need to go up! You need to get saved!"

But my passenger resisted and kept repeating, "I'm too drunk, I can't go now."

His friend continued to encourage him, "It doesn't matter, man! Go as you are! Jesus loves you! This is your time!" But he wouldn't go.

After the service, I drove the two friends to the corner diner for coffee and pie. The guy's friend told us he was recently saved, giving his life to Jesus. He explained how happy he was and that his life had improved since then. I shared the events of how God led me to pick him up and bring him to church. His friend marveled at the extent God had gone in answering his prayers.

It was evident I was no longer needed. My passenger was now in the good care of his old friend. I said good-bye and left them alone. Once outside I looked back through the window into the lit diner to see them hugging. What a joy to have been a part of God's redemptive plan, not only of my passenger, but also their reunion.

I looked for the two of them at church, but I never saw them again. I have often wondered what my passenger's story is from his perspective.

"Trust in the LORD with all your heart,
And lean not on your own understanding;
In all your ways acknowledge Him,
And He shall direct your paths."
Proverbs 3:5-6

MAN-HANDLED IN MAZATLÁN

God to the rescue

My cousin and I were vacationing in Mazatlán, Mexico when we were in our 20s. Our room was on the ground floor next to the pool. We often left our door open because we didn't have any valuables to worry about. The most expensive thing we took was our bathing suits and we were wearing them. We spent a lot of time around the pool fascinated by the interesting people we met from various places.

One afternoon, two hefty guys our age walked up and introduced themselves. Their accents and appearance revealed they were from the Mid-West. You know the type, large upper bodies with wide shoulders, muscular arms, and thick necks. They seemed like gentle souls, as nothing in their demeanor indicated we had any reason to be afraid of them.

However, when I went to our room one of them followed me in uninvited. I didn't notice him until he shoved me to the bed and jump on top of me. His large frame overcame me. All I could do was cry out, "Jesus, help me! Jesus, help me!"

As if someone grabbed him by the back of his plaid shirt, he was lifted off of me and thrown out the door. I didn't see anyone grab him. There wasn't anyone else in the room. I also didn't see him walk or run out on his own. He was just up and gone. I was unharmed but shaken by the experience, more overwhelmed by the powerful outcome.

I ran outside to where my cousin was lounging alone by the pool. I asked if she saw anyone enter or leave our room. She said she hadn't.

I have no explanation other than that Jesus came to my rescue when I cried out to Him for help, removing my attacker in a miraculous way. I have often wondered what that experience was like for him. I wonder what went through his mind when he encountered the mighty hand of God grab him from behind and toss him out the door. In the same way the intruder snuck up behind me with a forceful intent, God crept in and overpowered him with greater strength.

For whoever calls on the name of the LORD shall be saved.
Romans 10:13

"All my bones shall say, "LORD, who is like You,
Delivering the poor from him who is too strong for him,
Yes, the poor and the needy from him who plunders him?"
Psalm 35:10

This is the little house I lived in when my children were young. I experienced many wonderful encounters with God at this time. God taught me that the situations I found myself in weren't really about me. Instead they were created to reveal His power and presence in the midst of His people for Him glory. The following five stories occurred while living here.

SATURDAY BREAKFAST
God proves He is all-knowing and all-powerful

One Friday I tried to teach my children that God is all-knowing and all-powerful. But at age three, six and nine I realized this concept was hard for them to grasp. I gave up on explaining the meaning of the various Bible verses. Instead I simply told them that God knows what they're going to eat for breakfast the next morning.

Almost in unison they excitedly shouted, "Donuts!"

It was a Saturday morning tradition to visit the donut shop. They would hop in the van with their dad and reappear with a pink box of goodies while I made coffee. But their dad recently decided to stop visiting the donut shop on the premise it wasn't good for everyone's waistline. Trying to shield them from disappointment, I explained their dad probably wouldn't take them to the donut shop in the morning. Yet, I suggested we pray and see what God wants.

I prayed out loud with them, "Dear Lord, to prove You are all-knowing and all-powerful, we ask You to provide donuts for breakfast tomorrow. We agree donuts aren't good for our waistline, so please forgive us for such a frivolous prayer. Lord Your will is all we seek. Amen."

All three jumped up off the sofa, arms raised over their heads, shouting, "Hurray! We're having donuts tomorrow!"

It was wonderful seeing their faith in God, believing He would answer that prayer. "If God wills." I told them." Then I silently prayed, "Lord, help them to forget about this prayer so they won't be disappointed if donuts aren't in Your plan. Also, help them forget so they don't suggest the idea to their dad. Let them see You prove that You are all-knowing and all-powerful by supplying donuts." I had no idea what to expect. It was on my mind all day until the following morning. I knew God could prove to my children that He is all-powerful by providing donuts, but would He?

In the morning, I was the first one up. Next, the girls woke up, then the baby. Their dad was still asleep. We could hear him snoring in the bedroom. We sat in the living room together for a while until someone sleepily asked, "What's for breakfast?" It was obvious they had forgotten the prayer from the day before.

When I got up to prepare something to eat we heard a small muffled sentence from the bedroom that came at the tail end of a loud snore.

"What did you say?" one of the children shouted towards the bedroom.

"How 'bout donuts?" their dad repeated.

Then they remembered the prayer from the day before and ran in to tell their dad. Excitedly they got dressed and leaped into the van. Standing at the kitchen window I watched them drive off. I thanked God for creating an event that proved He is all-knowing and all-powerful in a tangible way my children understood. Overwhelmed by God's tender love for them, I was moved to tears.

"Great is our Lord and mighty in power; His understanding has no limit."
Psalm 147:5

WATCHING GOD
God at work

We could see everything in our part of the neighborhood in four directions. Our house was situated on a corner lot. We had the advantage of a schoolyard across the side street that extended our view. We also had the disadvantage of living across the street from the yellow house.

We didn't know the neighbors in the yellow house. I don't think anyone in the neighborhood knew them, or even wanted to. The house was the local hangout for teenage boys after school, which wasn't the problem. The trouble was, there didn't seem to be any parental supervision. The boys freely did as they pleased without any consequences. When they weren't causing trouble they typically skateboarded up and down the sidewalk until dark.

One week they sat on their roof, throwing rocks down on moving cars, scaring drivers. I remember the frightened look of an elderly woman as she suddenly braked from the loud noise that plummeted the roof of her car. The boys rolled in laughter from their high perch.

Another week, several times a day, their friend drove slowly through the neighborhood honking the car's horn. It was a continuous blast you could hear coming from the other end of the block until it loudly passed in front of the house before continuing to the opposite end of the street. They did this deliberately to annoy the neighborhood. All the other boys bent over laughing on the front lawn.

One afternoon the boys ganged up to pick on another boy in their group. Before he left for home, they gave him a large TV, the old boxy type. It seemed more like a joke than a gift. To get it home the boy put the TV on his skateboard and tried to roll it down the sidewalk. Each time he got the TV centered and moving, it fell off his narrow skateboard and scraped along the concrete. The other boys laughed at him without offering any help. It was obvious he was frustrated and embarrassed.

As I watched him through the windows a thought, not my own, came to mind, "You have a wagon." Believing this thought to be from the Lord, I walked out front to tell the boy I had a wagon he could borrow. He waited while I walked to the back yard to get it. As I walked through the house another thought, not my own, came to mind, "You have a minivan."

Instead of getting the wagon, I grabbed the car keys and invited my four-year-old son to ride along. In case the boy was afraid to accept the ride, I knew my young son, a natural socialite, would calm him, or at least entertain him while I drove. Plus, I wanted to show my son how to help others.

The boy was naturally apprehensive about getting into the van. I reassured him he'd be fine and I put my son in the front seat next to me. Since we weren't going far I told the boy he could sit in the back seat with the sliding side door left open. I promised to drive slowly. He agreed, put his TV in the back, then sat on the floor with his feet dangling out the door as we drove him home.

On the radio, a Christian song began to play. My son knew the lyrics, so he loudly sang along. I wondered if the boy had heard that song before. If not, did God use the lyrics to speak to him?

Could he see the joy my son was expressing and attribute it to God? Did God use our actions to prove He cared for him?

I don't know the answers to these questions. I only did what God asked me to do. I'm sure God didn't enjoy watching the boy being picked on any more than I did. Secretly, I hoped the boy saw that people who follow Jesus act differently than those who were heckling him. I also hoped the other boys noticed the kindness that contradicted their actions. I was glad God prompted me to help him with a ride where he was able to hear God being praised through song. Wagons don't have radios.

When I read Jesus' words in Matthew 25:35-36, *"For I was hungry and you gave Me food; I was thirsty and you gave Me drink; I was a stranger and you took Me in; I was naked and you clothed Me; I was sick and you visited Me; I was in prison and you came to Me..."* I wonder if that also includes, "I needed a ride and you drove me."

"Bear one another's burdens,
and so fulfill the law of Christ."
Galatians 6:2

ENCHILADAS

If your enemy hungers feed him

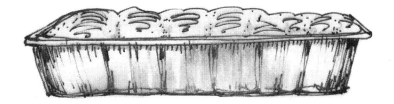

I read a story to my children that taught the Biblical principle of loving your enemies. The story told of three brothers who were being mistreated by neighbor boys who threw dirt clods at them. The youngest brother ran up to the house and asked his mom for some cookies, which she gave him. In turn, this young boy gave the cookies to the neighbor bullies and said, "You must be hungry after throwing all those dirt clods at us." That act convicted the bullies and they stopped being unkind. Later in the story, all the boys became friends.

I remember thinking that's a very nice story to teach children, but I'm not sure that's how I would have reacted. Remember our neighbor boys in the last story, who threw rocks at cars, scaring drivers? That's not the only thing they threw. Several times an open bottle of grass killer was thrown on our lawn.

My six-year-old daughter, on the other hand, took this story to heart. She suggested we make snickerdoodle cookies for our neighbor bullies. I was impressed with her suggestion and she loved making snickerdoodles, so that's what we did. But when the cookies were done I didn't suggest taking any over to the neighbors. Instead we ate all of them. Mainly because I was too afraid to take them to the boys next door. Yet I felt terrible, like God was saying to me, "That wasn't good enough."

Throughout the day I was conflicted. Did I miss an opportunity to do something God wanted me to do? I was happy helping the underdog with his TV from the previous story. I wasn't comfortable giving a bunch of hooligans a treat. It felt like I was rewarding their bad behavior.

While making dinner the following day it felt like God was telling me, "You have more than enough ingredients to make extra Enchiladas for the boys across the street."

I halfheartedly gave God a curt answer, "OK, but the boys never came home from school today. They better be home at 5:30 when these are ready." I was stubbornly giving God an ultimatum in order for me to comply with His request. I hoped the boys wouldn't be home in time and I would to be relieved of my obligation. I was afraid of their maliciousness.

As the enchiladas baked in the oven, I watched to see if the boys arrived at home. When the oven timer beeped I was relieved I never saw them. I took the first tray out and set it on the counter. While taking the second tray out of the oven I heard a large group of boys hollering at each other. It was the neighbors and their friends. They ran across their front lawn, unlocked the front door, and scrambled inside.

My heart was heavy because I was now more afraid of God than those He wanted me to give the enchiladas to. I put foil over the top of their tray and told my children to stay inside. I walked up their front steps and knocked on the door. The door opened a only a crack, enough to see half of a boy's face. He was surprised to see me.

I was nervous. I blurted out a few short sentences. "I made these enchiladas for you. They are delicious. You must be hungry. I know you want them." All the while I continuously shook my head up and down gesturing, "Yes!" I had to convince him to take them. I couldn't go home empty-handed. I didn't want to have to do this again.

He opened the screen door wide enough to put his hand out and pull the tray in sideways before he slammed the door. I pictured all the warm enchiladas sliding to one side of the tray. Relieved of my duties I ran home. It didn't occur to me anything would come from it.

The next day a woman knocked on my front door. She introduced herself as the boy's mom in the yellow house. She thanked us for the enchiladas and brought us a tray of cookies, what we were supposed to deliver the first time. We invited her in and she told us her story.

She was a single mom who felt bad she couldn't be home for her boys, as she needed to work. The boy's father was a police officer who spent little time with them. The boys learned they could make trouble and their dad would use his influence to get them out of it. She thought they acted out as a way to get their dad's attention. She said it made the boys angry when they saw my children playing in the front yard with their dad. Since they didn't experience that, they acted out against us. She promised the boys would stop, and they did.

It helped me to know their story. I would have never been able to turn my anger into empathy had I not pushed through my own fear to obey God. I learned the fear I was experiencing came from the enemy. Fear is a tactic the devil uses to hinder us from obeying God, and blessing others. I also learned that the hunger our enemy feels may not be a hunger for food. In this case, the neighbor boys were hungry for their father's time and affection.

"If your enemy is hungry, give him food to eat; if he is thirsty, give him water to drink. In doing this, you will heap burning coals on his head, and the LORD will reward you." Proverbs 25:21-22

FIVE DOLLARS

God supplies every need

At the last minute, a friend invited me to hear Zvi Kalisher speak at a church that evening. We would need to leave right away to get there in time. I asked if I needed money because I didn't have any cash. She said she didn't think so and hoped not because she didn't have any cash either.

Zvi shared how God miraculously saved him from the Holocaust when he was a boy. Then he told how he came to believe in Jesus. Finally, he shared how God opens opportunities for him to share the gospel with his Jewish neighbors in Israel. If you have an opportunity to read his book or watch a video of him telling his story, I highly recommend them.

At the end of his talk, the church took an offering for Zvi. I was disappointed I didn't have anything to share. A prompting of the Holy Spirit encouraged me to look in my wallet for something to give him. But I ignored the prodding, as I already knew I didn't have any cash. Yet, God continued to nag me to look in my wallet. I finally relented thinking I may have a few coins.

I remember feeling like the widow giving her last two mites, and I asked God to increase the small amount I may find. But I didn't have any coins. I searched the slot for dollars hoping to find a misplaced coin there but instead I found a $5 bill. I know it wasn't there before because I looked in my wallet when my friend called.

When the offering basket was handed to me I added the $5 bill. My friend gave me an inquisitive look as if to say, "I thought you said you didn't have any cash." I shrugged my shoulders and told her I didn't, and believe God put it there for me to give.

Early the next morning one of my children asked if they could have some money. I told them I didn't have any cash on me. I was combated with, "Just look in your wallet, Mom." I opened my wallet to prove it was empty but instead I found another $5 bill.

Of course, I have no logical explanation for how the money miraculously appeared in my wallet twice. It's similar to the story of a coin found in a fish's mouth as told in Matthew 17:24-27. Jesus told Peter to catch a fish and in it he would find the money to pay the temple tax. I'm sure Peter was as surprised at his finding as I was with mine.

I want to encourage you. If you are a child of the living God, a follower of Jesus, yielded to the leading of the Holy Spirit, why wouldn't God surprise you with His miraculous handiwork. We are His children after all, and He loves us. Like a good Father He wants to interact with us. He wants us to experience Him.

"And my God will liberally supply your every need
according to His riches in glory in Christ Jesus."
Philippians 4:19

TINY TREASURE
God delivers joy

We were in Colorado for a family reunion. For some reason, my ten-year-old daughter didn't want to go on a scheduled hike in the woods along a stream. Leaving her alone in the hotel room wasn't an option. We got her in the car and to the trailhead, but she lagged behind as the group made their way to the destination. I lagged behind with her trying to spark her interest in joining the others without success.

Giving up, I silently prayed, "Lord I'm out of ideas, please encourage her to want to join the others and to have a fun day." I honestly didn't know what to expect. I was frustrated we weren't hiking with the rest of the family

Moments later she saw something move on the trail. Following the movements in the grass, she discovered a tiny frog. She picked it up and excitedly showed it to me. The image of it cupped in her little hands will forever be burned in my memory. For at that moment God lifted her spirits and gave her joy.

With much enthusiasm, she wanted to show the others her tiny treasure. With the frog gently cupped in her hands she ran ahead to catch up with the group. Now I was trying to keep up with her on the trail.

Whatever her reason for previously lagging behind, I was glad I stayed with her. I had the privilege of witnessing God encouraged her in a marvelous way.

"You will show me the path of life;
In Your presence is fullness of joy;
At Your right hand are pleasures forevermore."
Psalm 16:11

This is the home God moved my family into next. When I first saw it for sale I thought, "That's an ugly green house," and drove past it. The dead grass was pale yellow, and the cactus plants were dried up. The only green was the paint on the house and it was pealing.

But God said, "Move to the land I show you," and He showed me the ugly green house again.

It needed everything. After I moved in I heard comments like, "What are your hopes and dreams?" or "So you're the one who bought the ugly green house." And my favorite being, "My mom looked at that house and said to my dad, 'There's no way I'm living there.'"

I learned from living here that a house isn't anything, really. Only a 2x4 frame covered in various materials. God blessed us with the resources to remodel the structure, but it's people who were the real treasure in God's eyes. I thank Him for revealing that part of His heart to me.

LOVE NOTES
God's heart revealed

Have you ever had an idea that initially seemed good but later made you nervous to actually do it? I've discovered these are the ideas God plants in our heart to deliver a blessing. The nervousness we feel is typically from the enemy meant to thwart God's work.

Such a moment happened just before the first Valentine's Day in our new neighborhood. The idea was simply to make a card for each neighbor to express God's love for them. What made me nervous was to include a Bible verse on each card. I was worried the scripture would be met with opposition.

I doodled a little garden of heart-shaped flowers and pushed past the thought of any criticism a Bible verse might bring. I choose 1 John 4:16,

> "And we have known and believed the love that God has for us. God is love, and he who abides in love abides in God, and God in him."

Seventy cards were copied, one for each house in the neighborhood. My children helped put each card in a cellophane bag with a few heart-shaped chocolates to sweeten the gift. A ribbon was added as a doorknob hanger. Together we marched through the neighborhood delivering our wagon of gifts.

It wasn't long afterward we met other believers in our neighborhood. Most surprising, though, was the blessing our gift became to the elderly widows. They hadn't received a Valentine card in several years. It was apparent God was especially reaching out His tender heart toward them. The joy they experienced from that tiny gift far exceeded any assumed opposition, of which there wasn't any.

CHICKENS MUST GO
God rewards sacrifice

When God requires something to be given up, there is always a greater reward received then what we want to hold on to. The problem is we love that which we are required to relinquish.

I loved my chickens. The three we currently had where named Shirley, Goodness, and Mercy because they followed us around the yard wherever we went. They were our pets.

Our new neighbors did not love them. Early every morning our chickens loudly called out from the yard to be fed. Later in the day they took turns cackling as one of them laid her egg. I think it's a defense tactic to distract a predator away from the laying hen. Several times I heard my neighbor over the fence complain, "Ahh, those chickens again!"

The Lord kept asking me, "What's more important, your neighbor or your chickens?" I didn't know my neighbor very well, so I didn't answer His question.

I learned it didn't matter to God how well I knew my neighbor. His next question was, "Did I die for the soul of your neighbor or your chickens?"

I couldn't ignore this question; I knew what He meant. It was better to live in peace with my neighbor than live within my right to have chickens. Though I loved my chickens, I also needed to love my neighbor. As Christ freely gave Himself to be a sacrifice on our behalf, I needed to be Christlike to my neighbor. Shirley, Goodness, and Mercy were given to a friend who lived further out of town.

After the chickens were gone my neighbor asked if she could join us at church. A visiting pastor spoke the day she came. After his message, he gave the invitation to receive Jesus as Lord and Savior. My neighbor accepted the invitation and went forward for prayer.

The sacrifice I made was well worth it. Sitting in the back row at church I began to cry. I always cry when souls accept Jesus as their Savior, but this time I cried more than usual. Crying is also a sign the Lord is calling you to Himself, a realization that you need Him, that you need to be saved.

The visiting pastor noticed me crying and wiping my tears on the sleeve of my sweater. He mistook my joy for the need of salvation and continued calling, "I believe there is one more in the back of the room. The Lord is calling you. Come and receive His salvation. Come now for He is waiting for you."

The pastor seemed disappointed I didn't respond to his call. I had already given my life to Christ. Metaphorically speaking, I recently gave Christ my chickens. In response to my minuscule sacrifice, Jesus did a work in my neighbor's heart that was possible because of His ultimate sacrifice.

"Do not lay up for yourselves treasures on earth, where moth and rust destroy and where thieves break in and steal; but lay up for yourselves treasures in heaven, where neither moth nor rust destroy and where thieves do not break in and steal.
Matthew 6:19-20

CUT OFF

God opens opportunities

Three young boys were sitting in the back seat of my car when it happened. It was Monday morning in the middle of Summer. I was driving to Church for the first day of Vacation Bible School where I volunteered to help with arts and crafts. My young son wanted to attend and invited two of his friends from our neighborhood.

We were driving on I-5 crossing over Encinitas Boulevard. A young man abruptly swerved in front of us into our lane. I had to quickly break to avoid hitting his car. My first thought was to yell at him even though I knew he couldn't hear me. A quick look in the rearview mirror revealed three startled faces. It took me a while to think of an appropriate response. I definitely didn't want to set a bad example for my son or his two guests.

The thought came to mind to pray out loud for the young man now driving in front of us. I don't remember exactly what I prayed, but it was something to the effect of asking God to protect and guide him and to lead him to salvation in Jesus.

My son and his friends enjoyed VBS, so on Tuesday morning we returned to church. In the same place on the freeway where the first guy swerved in front of us, a different guy in a different car also cut us off. So as before, I prayed for him out loud, repeating the same prayer the first guy received.

Wednesday morning in the same place, we were cut off by a third guy on the freeway. I know it's hard to believe, I hardly believed it myself at the time. The driver in front of us received the same prayer as the first two.

This is a God story, so beyond my comprehension, it happened twice more in the same place on the freeway. Two additional guys cut us off, one on Thursday morning and another on Friday morning. As before, the boys sitting in the back seat of my car agreed we should pray and ask God to protect, guide, and lead them to salvation in Jesus also.

I'm thankful God provided the interruptions that opened an opportunity to teach three young boys to pray for others. I'm personally hoping five young men found salvation in Jesus because they cut us off on I-5 in Encinitas the week of Vacation Bible School. I hope to meet them personally someday, if not in this life, then in the one to come.

"Train up a child in the way he should go,
And when he is old he will not depart from it."
Proverbs 22:6

CROSSING PATHS

God gives us words to say

I just stepped into the market to get a few things for dinner. After I grabbed a small hand basket, a young man walked towards me a bit agitated. He looked like he was in a hurry and couldn't find what he was looking for. He was dressed up, wearing a black blazer over a black shirt, and black pants. The only thing that wasn't black was a large gold cross that hung on a long thick gold chain over his black tie. He stopped and stood right in front of me. He was too busy looking for something else to notice I was standing in front of him. God interrupted my thoughts with, "Ask him what his cross means to him."

I ignored the suggestion doubting it was God talking to me. The young man then turned around and walked to the other side of the store. Then my heart burned inside me from the conviction of not obeying God. I remained in the same place contemplating if I should go after him. Then he turned around and walked back towards me looking down each aisle for what he was searching for.

Having walked back the width of the store, this time he noticed me, but only because I was obstructing his way.

As he stood in front of me God repeated His instruction, "Ask him now!"

I blurted out, "What does your cross mean to you?"

Irritated, he replied in a curt tone, "What?"

This time I said, "God wants me to ask you what your cross means to you." I couldn't imagine what he was thinking, for what I said sounded ridiculous to me. What a bold question to ask someone you don't know.

He was obviously stunned and momentarily lost for words, and then calmly replied, "I just like wearing it." I could tell his countenance had changed. He stopped being hurried; instead he looked somber and still before turning away from me.

It's an uncomfortable feeling when God asks you to do something that doesn't make sense. I don't know what those words meant to him. They must have been important for God to make us cross paths in the market, to convict me of not asking him the question the first time, and to redirect him to stand in front of me a second time. I remember wondering if God used others to ask him the same question as a way of calling him to the Savior. I hope I see him again, if not here on earth then in God's heavenly kingdom.

If God instructs you to boldly speak out to a stranger, I encourage you to do so. Don't worry if it doesn't make sense or how weird it may seem. God is doing something miraculous in that person's life and in yours. We don't need to know the outcome, it's God's work and He does everything for His grand purpose.

"For we are His workmanship, created in Christ Jesus for good works, which God prepared beforehand that we should walk in them."
Ephesians 2:10

TEA TIME

God always wins

Have you ever committed to help someone, only to later regret you had done so? This is one such event. Even though I no longer wanted to attend this tea party, God had other plans.

An elderly woman at my church wanted to host a tea party at her house. It was her way of thanking all the women at from church who helped her after her husband passed away. She asked me to help set it up. I offered to bring an assortment of teas and a large hot water pot for brewing.

She called me almost every day to ask how to arrange the tables, what foods to prepare, and how to serve a large group. I suggested different options for her to choose from. This is when I discovered she swore a lot. Every sentence spoken with cuss words. It shocked me at first. I had never heard an elderly woman at church talk like that. The more I spoke with her, the more it escalated, and the more uncomfortable I became. I no longer wanted to go to her tea party, but I couldn't back out, I was bringing the tea.

On the day of the tea party I was the first to arrive at her house. I needed to heat the water and set up a tea display before the others arrived. I left my purse locked in the car and carried in the tea, hot water pot, and my car keys. I set my keys on a tall stool at the end of the kitchen counter. It was warm inside, so I took off my sweater and set it on the stool on top of my keys.

As the guests arrived, the elderly woman gave tours of her home and art studio. I didn't know she was an artist, so I followed the other guests down the hall. She spoke about her house, her artwork, and family. As she did, she peppered her sentences with cuss words. It appeared the other women from my church were also uncomfortable. They each excused themselves from her studio until I alone was with her.

Curious, I asked her, "Why do you cuss all the time?"

To which she replied, "To shock the churchy ladies. I just want to shock them out of being such goody goods."

It was intentional? Remember, these are the "good" women who helped her in her time of need. That's when I realized the Spirit of God may not be in her even though she went to church. Her actions appeared mean-spirited and unthankful. Repulsed by it, I planned to leave her tea party as soon as possible.

One guest who arrived late had a difficult time finding a parking place on the steep road next her house. She accidentally backed her car into a deep drainage ditch, unable to get out of it.

I offered to call AAA to help her, but my keys were no longer on the stool under my sweater. I needed my keys to unlock my car to get the AAA card in my purse. Since I was no help, someone else called a tow truck as I frantically looked elsewhere for my car keys. Unable to find my keys I second-guessed myself and thought I must have locked them in the car. After the tow truck driver pulled my friend's car out of the ditch he kindly unlocked my car. But searching my car and purse, my keys were not there.

I went back inside and sat at one of the small tables. I silently prayed, asking God to help me find my keys. I felt God tell me He had taken my keys and hidden them. I became angry, in my mind I argued with God. I told Him I was uncomfortable being there and wanted to leave as soon as possible. I didn't understand why He wanted me to stay.

I sensed Him say, "I want you to wash her dishes."

In my mind I argued back, "No, I don't want to, I want to leave. Don't make me wash her dishes."

God's rebuttal was, "Wash her dishes or I won't give you your keys."

My friend sitting across the table from me noticed my disappointment and asked if I was all right. I told her I was arguing with God. Being a very spiritual person, she replied, "God always wins." I knew she was right.

I don't recall much about the party, except the numerous times I got up to see if my keys were on the stool under my sweater. We ate, drank tea, and the elderly woman told stories about her late husband. As her guests began to leave, I wanted to leave too. I wanted to be at home with my children, but there was something God wanted me to do first.

Checking one last time for my keys on the stool under my sweater without success, I began washing her dishes. She was busy clearing tables and removing table cloths. As I looked around, there were no other women there. No one stayed to help her clean up afterward as is typically done among Christian women. I didn't blame them; they probably felt as I did.

Seeing her clearing tables by herself made me feel sorry for her. She went to church, she heard the word of God, and she witnessed these women help her in her time of need. Yet it appeared she harbored a mean spirit towards them. That spirit drove them off and left her alone.

With an armful of table cloths, she came and stood next to me and asked, "Why are you washing my dishes?"

The words that came out of my mouth were not my own, for I would have said something totally different. Instead, the Holy Spirit took control of my mouth and out came the words, "Because Jesus loves you."

She didn't reply but simply walked away. I continued to wash her dishes, and when I was finished, I found my keys under my sweater on the stool where I originally set them.

I can't explain how this happened, but I do know why. God had an important message He wanted the elderly woman to hear. She needed to know He loved her.

"Therefore, my beloved,
as you have always obeyed,
not as in my presence only,
but now much more in my absence,
work out your own salvation with fear and trembling;
for it is God who works in you both to will and
to do for His good pleasure."
Philippians 2:12-13

PICNIC TABLE
God provides

I was on the search for a large picnic table to put in the backyard. I wanted one large enough for my three children and their friends to sit around. Nearby stores carried a variety of sturdy tables, all out of my price range. Tables in my price range were flimsy that wouldn't hold up to the weather and use. I decided to pray. I simply told God it would be nice to have a picnic table. If it was in His will for us to have one I asked Him to lead me to one that I could afford.

Three days later a young man knocked on my front door. He introduced himself and asked if I needed a picnic table, pointing to his flatbed truck parked by the curb. It was full of unfinished wood tables with long benches he and his father made. I told him I was amazed to see him standing on my porch, as three days earlier I prayed asking God to lead me to a picnic table I could afford. He was equally surprised because he was also a believer. He came from a long distance to deliver custom chairs to a store nearby. While in the area he decided to see if anyone else needed a picnic table or chairs.

He said if I bought one of his tables with two benches he would throw in a loveseat, two side chairs and an end table for $100. It was the exact amount I could afford and told him I'd take the set. He was so happy that he asked if he could pray to give God the glory. That picnic table set was painted different colors over the years and lasted long after my children were grown.

"Seek the Kingdom of God above all else,
and He will give you everything you need."
Luke 12:31 NLT

SURFBOARD BLESSING
God blesses those who obey Him

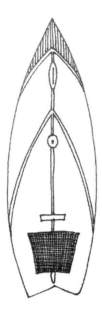

My son was being difficult. I don't remember how old he was, but I remember he was old enough to stay home alone. This I remember because I needed to go shopping and didn't want to take him with me.

Yet, I had a deep sense God was telling me to take him with me wherever I needed to go that day, and to keep him near. I believed this thought was from God because I would have never thought it on my own. I also had the impression God was telling me that he would continue to be difficult, which he was. I felt God coaching me to remain calm throughout the day, to not let his stubbornness win, remain firm, and above all, use that time to teach him God's word. Deuteronomy 30:19 was his favorite verse at the time, so I decided to reinforce its teaching. The verse reads,

> "I call heaven and earth as witnesses today against you, that I have set before you life and death, blessing and cursing, therefore choose life, that you and your descendants may live."

More than once I repeated the verse hoping to show him that the outcome of his day was based on his choices. He remained challenging. It wasn't fun. Finally, at 3:30 in the grocery store he took a deep breath, apologized for his behavior and became pleasant.

We arrived home at 4:00. He was carrying grocery bags to the kitchen when the phone rang. He answered it. It was his dad calling to tell him that someone had given him a surfboard, and he was bringing it home. It belonged to a friend's son who had outgrown it, which was now perfectly suited for his age. He put the phone aside to tell me the good news. I asked him to ask his dad what time the surfboard was given. He said, "Thirty minutes ago."

Did you catch that? Thirty minutes earlier was 3:30. At the exact moment my son made the choice to change, God provided a gift for him. Remember his verse? *"I have set before you ... blessing and cursing; therefore choose..."* He chose, and God blessed!

When God spoke to me earlier that morning He didn't speak in an audible voice, only a thought, so I wasn't sure I actually heard Him. I acted on faith of what I believed to be the leading of the Holy Spirit. It wasn't until the outcome of the event that I knew for sure it was Him I heard. God wasn't only teaching my son a lesson, He was also teaching me to better hear and obey His voice even when it wasn't convenient or comfortable to do so.

God has blessings stored up for those who honor Him. It isn't easy to obey, even as an adult. It takes faith and trust to follow God's leading. The more we yield to Him, the easier it becomes to discern His voice. When we become part of His plan we witness His handiwork and reap a blessing. What blessing did I receive that day? I witnessed God blessing my son for making the right choice.

"Oh, how great is Your goodness, which You have laid up
for those who fear You, which You have prepared for those
who trust in You in the presence of the sons of men!"
Psalm 31:19

CHRISTMAS GREETINGS

God won't share His glory

I procrastinated painting a new Christmas greeting card for work. One was needed but I put it off till the last minute, choosing to paint other designs ahead of it. I was also over ambitious trying to design and watercolor eight new cards in a short period of time. After painting the seventh card I was drained of ideas and exhausted from staying up late to meet my deadline.

I decided to walk around the block and pray. First, I repented for leaving what was needed for last and for becoming exhausted by filling my time with other things. Then I asked God for an idea for a Christmas card, one that would please and glorify Him. He began to fill my mind with images of shepherds and an angel on a teacup. A star was over the angel with shadows cast in an outward direction from the star. Sheep were in a field on the saucer and a manager in the foreground. In the background behind the teacup, an image of a town representing Bethlehem came to mind.

With new enthusiasm, I returned to my studio. I created a little sketch and began painting. When I was finished I mounted it on the wall next to the other new cards, stepped back for a look, and proclaimed out loud, "Wow! I'm amazing!"

With my tasks for the season complete, I returned to my desk to clean up. Feeling puffed up from my accomplishments, walking with an over-exuberant stride, my foot stumbled on the leg of my desk. I was quickly pitched off balance. My head abruptly slammed onto the tabletop. I can still remember how it felt with my glasses embedded into the side of my face.

As I lay there catching my breath, a still, small voice spoke to my heart. It asked, "Who's amazing?"

Lesson learned. I felt awful because I knew my inspiration came from God. He is eager to help us in every area of our lives. Yet, He won't let us take credit for what He has done, and rightly so. He deserves all the honor and glory for the marvelous work He does in our lives. And when we do mess up, He is so willing to forgive us our faults as we confess them.

"Pride goes before destruction,
a haughty spirit before a fall."
Proverbs 16:18

SUITE CONFRONTATION
God's difficult instruction

An available suite across the parking lot looked appealing to me. It was larger than my current office space that I was growing out of. If I would have known ahead of time what God would ask me to do after I inquired about the newly available space, I would have remained where I was. But God rarely tells us in advance what He requires of us.

Before calling the property manager I first prayed to ask God if it was His will for me to relocate. As I sat in the front window praying, looking across the parking lot to the other suite, praise music softly played in the background. The chorus repeatedly sang, "Je-sus, Oh Je-e-e-sus."

A thought came to mind, "Look at the suite number across the parking lot." It was suite J. J as in Jesus? I felt like God was saying, "You are now in suite G, G for God. Moving to Suite J, for Jesus, would be feasible." I know that sounds silly, but there was an assurance God was answering my prayer and a promise He would take care of the extra expense of the larger Suite. Seven years earlier

God led me to Suite G. He miraculously provided the deposit to move in, and then continued to provide the income for rent.

I called the property manager to ask about the vacant suite. He was a classic salesman with flattering words that may cause some to question if the truth was fully told. He came to my office to meet with me the following day, bringing with him a young woman, his new assistant. He noticed the poster in our window advertising a local revival meeting. He then professed to be a Christian and said his children went to a nearby Christian School.

After telling him about my interest in relocating to the larger suite, he misquoted the terms of my current lease agreement followed by a list of obstacles that hindered me from relocating to the larger space. He chuckled trying to be convincing, than gave his assistant a wink as if their spiel was rehearsed. She reemphasized his remarks with a nod, but I wasn't convinced. Disturbed he may be deceiving me, I asked him to validate his statements, which he couldn't do.

I was bothered the rest of the day thinking the property manager may be lying to me. I asked God to show me scripture in the Bible to help me make sense of why I was so upset. I was led to read 1 Timothy chapter 4:1-6,

> "Now the Spirit expressly says that in latter times some will depart from the faith, giving heed to deceiving spirits and doctrines of demons, speaking lies in hypocrisy, having their own conscience seared with a hot iron . . . If you instruct the brethren in these things, you will be a good minister of Jesus Christ, nourished in the words of faith and of the good doctrine which you have carefully followed."

These verses shed some light on why people lie, but now I was faced with a new challenge. I strongly felt God wanted me to address him about lying. I struggled with this. I wasn't comfortable confronting him. He was an adult and had the right to his own choices. Yet, along with the urgency to talk to him, God revealed the error of a lying Christian that misrepresents God to others.

The next morning, I shared God's specific instruction with my office assistant. She was a former missionary and I was looking for affirmation to obey God's word. However, she was absolutely against it and her opposition surprised me. I would have gladly heeded her advice and avoided the conversation. I didn't want to call him. Yet my conviction from God to talk to the property manager was more powerful than her advice or my desire to avoid doing it.

I went into my office and shut the door and called the property manager. I told him I was calling on a personal matter and asked if he had a moment to talk. He said he did. I told him what I observed the day before. I shared the verses God led me to read, and suggested he had two options. He either had to stop telling people he was a Christian or stop lying. To combine the two misrepresents God, especially to an impressionable young assistant. He said he couldn't stop telling people he was a Christian. Then I suggested he needed to stop lying. He was obviously upset by my call. I didn't blame him because I hated making the call.

Then something weird happened. Previous to our conversation, I rarely saw the property manager at the office complex, and I never saw him anywhere else. However, the following week I saw him every day around town. First, he ran across the street in front of my car wearing jogging clothes. I had to brake to miss him, and he looked directly at me inside my car as he ran to get out of the way. Then I saw him at the market. We were standing in the same checkout line. I can't remember where else I saw him around town, but it was obvious God was causing those interactions to happen because each time we were both surprised to see the other.

In the weeks that that followed I could tell a change was happening within him. He often came to my office just to say hello. It became a well-known phrase from my staff, "Hey Kim, your buddy is here to see you." Though he never said anything about our telephone conversation, his demeanor became happier and there was more joy in his face. I could see the change God was doing in his heart that began with a very hard telephone call. In the end, I was glad for God's strong conviction that prodded me to talk to him. I looked forward to his visits at the larger Suite J every now and then just to say hello.

The times when God asked me to do something very difficult, I notice He already created the successful outcome of my obedience. The key to living a life yielded to Christ is to follow Him, to go where He leads, to obey His commands, and to do what He asks. We need to not be afraid. Fear is not of God. Fear is a diversion tactic of the enemy used to thwart God's redemptive plans. Do not give into fear and see the wondrous acts of God in your life and those in your sphere of influence.

"Brethren, if anyone among you wanders from the truth, and someone turns him back, let him know that he who turns a sinner from the error of his way will save a soul from death and cover a multitude of sins."
James 5:19-20

THE DONKEY
God works through trials

These intertwining stories each began with a trial. A **friend** needed a car. A **neighbor** needed to sell one. My friend's situation was grim. Both of her cars had broken down and her husband lost his job. To make things worse, they were told they needed to move from the home they were renting, as it would be sold. Her family was living on their son's fast-food income and the generosity of those led by the Lord to share. Simultaneously my neighbor was having trouble selling her minivan. The sale would provide for needs her family had.

The outcome of this story would not be possible unless I previously had my own trial. The mighty hand of God caused the win of a trademark infringement of my greeting cards. It was a miraculous event where God asked me to trust Him, believing on faith that He is "Wonderful, Counselor, Mighty God, Everlasting Father, Prince of Peace," as described in Isaiah 9:6.

Lawyers are often called a counselor. God said to me, "You don't need a lawyer, I am your Counselor," and He was. By trusting God, I won a settlement without lawyers or going to court. During my involvement with this trademark-infringing company, God led me to a verse that was more like a promise, priming me for what He was going to ask me to do afterwards. The verse was Proverbs 28:8. It reads,

"One who increases his possessions by usury and extortion,
Gathers it for him who will pity the poor."

As a result, I had the resources to help my friend and my neighbor at the same time. God instructed me to buy my neighbor's minivan and give it to my friend.

Before God instructed me to give the minivan to my friend, He spoke to her heart. At church, she heard the teaching about the donkey Jesus rode on into Jerusalem. During that message, God revealed that He was going to provide transportation for her as well. That's how the minivan came to be called, "The Donkey."

I approached my neighbor about buying her minivan and explained it would be given to someone else who needed it. I later learned my neighbor's mom doubted that God existed until then. Seeing how God led one person to meet the need of another reinforced her mom's faith that God was real.

My friend's husband also doubted God's existence. Having just lost his job, with two cars broken down, and the unexpected need to move, I didn't blame him. I had been in his shoes before and knew how he felt. The Donkey began to renew his faith that there was a God who cared for him and his family.

Shortly after The Donkey was delivered to its new home, my friend called to say the transmission went out. I told her not to worry. The Donkey just threw a shoe and I'd have it fixed. I called AAA to have it towed to a shop. I then met the tow truck driver at my friend's house, left my car for her to use, and planned to ride with the driver to the repair shop.

The tow truck driver was a large muscular Samoan man. My friend looked worried and whispered, "Aren't you nervous about getting in the truck with him?" I wasn't until she said it. But then I rethought the whole series of events that led up to this point. God always completes what He starts. It didn't seem feasible He would end this gifting by putting me in danger.

Once the minivan was hitched and ready to go, I hopped in the cab with the driver. The driver asked what happened to the van. I sensed the Holy Spirit say, "Tell him the entire story." I wasn't sure he would understand all the things God had done involving this van, but I told him anyway. As I shared the story he became noticeably happier and full of joy.

With a big smile he said, "That's an amazing story! My dad is the pastor of the Samoan Christian church and I can't wait to tell everyone. They're going to be really blessed."

In the end, it was obvious every detail of this story was the work of God. Through the sale of one minivan God provided the immediate need of two families at the same time. God also used the sale of the van to develop a mom's new faith in Him, as well as rekindle a husband's faith. With renewed faith, God blessed my friend's husband with a new job that came with a company car, and the extra income allowed them to purchase their own home. As a bonus, God also revealed this story to the Samoan Christian church, blessing them with evidence of how God works in the midst of His people. For me, God taught a new attribute about Him. He is our Wonderful Counselor who is able to use trials to encourage His people, expand His kingdom, and bring glory to His name.

"My brethren, count it all joy when you fall into various trials,
knowing that the testing of your faith produces patience.
But let patience have its perfect work, that you may be perfect
and complete, lacking nothing. If any of you lacks wisdom,
let him ask of God, who gives to all liberally and
without reproach, and it will be given to him."
James 1:2-5

REALLY BIG

God proves He is real

I was in front of my house chatting with a neighbor on the sidewalk when another neighbor, Rebecca, walked over to join us. We must have been talking about God because Rebecca asked us, "How do you know God is real?" I shared verses from the Bible, but Rebecca wasn't convinced. She repeated, "But HOW do you know?" After I told her the story of Jesus, Rebecca asked again, "BUT, HOW do you know Jesus is the way to God, not Buddha, or Mohammad or..." she continued listing other religious leaders.

Finally, I told her what I did when I didn't know either. I said, "I figured if Jesus was real and He was God, He was fully capable of proving it. So, I asked Him to prove to me He was real, and He did."

"OK!" she said, "But it better be REALLY BIG!" and walked back home.

A week later Rebecca suffered from severe headaches and confused speech. She was diagnosed with a brain tumor, rushed to the hospital, and operated on shortly after. She was told the operation would impair her vision, hearing, and speech.

I was at the hospital thirty minutes after her surgery. I wasn't able to visit her in her room, but I watched down the hall as her family wept with joy. They told me Rebecca could see, hear and speak normally.

When Rebecca was settled in at home I went to visit her. She reminded me of the conversation we had in front of my house. She said she had made her peace with God before going into surgery. To prove God was real, she asked Him to allow her to see, hear and speak normally after her tumor was removed. That was the "REALLY BIG" way God could prove to her that He was real, and Jesus was the way. As a result, she gave her life to Christ and became a believer.

"Ah, Lord GOD! Behold,
You have made the heavens and the earth
by Your great power and outstretched arm.
There is nothing too hard for You."
Jeremiah 32:17

TOO TIRED TO TRAVEL
Angel in charge

It was 2am as I drove south on Hwy 5 through Camp Pendleton. We had been driving for ten hours, returning home from relatives in northern CA to celebrate Thanksgiving. The rest of my family in the car was naturally sound asleep.

I could see the Oceanside pier in the distance lit up over the ocean. It had always served as a beacon signaling we were almost home, but I had trouble keeping my eyes open. I just passed a sign indicating a rest stop was one mile ahead. For safety's sake, I considered stopping to sleep for a while, but it seemed pointless when I was only 15 minutes from home.

I prayed, "God, please help me stay awake so I can get us home safely." A second later something caught my eye in the right rear-view mirror. It was a small figure in the shape of a person silhouetted by headlights a long distance behind. The small figure was next to the right rear fender. It was suspended in the air, traveling along at the same speed as our vehicle, wearing a long robe down to their feet. I couldn't see any detail, only a silhouette.

Startled by the sight I yelled out loud, "Oh, my God!" My shout woke up everyone except the youngest that was in the third-row seat. I was now wide-awake. God had used the presence of what I believe to be an angel to jolt me out of my sleepiness and reassure me I was in His care. Fifteen minutes later we arrived home safely.

"For He shall give His angels charge over you,
to keep you in all your ways."
Psalm 91:11

CHEESECAKE

God treats us with His sense of humor

I was frustrated with being overweight. I asked God to help me overcome my weight gain with this prayer, "Dear God, I'm sorry I let myself get fat. I'm sorry for mistreating my body that You created. Please take away my desire for all foods that are not good for me, actually make me hate them. But as an occasional treat, may I please have a piece of cheesecake, but only when someone offers it to me." It was a Thursday. I didn't share my prayer with anyone.

I was committed to losing weight, eating healthier, and to never again buy cheesecake. The conclusion of my prayer was simply to allow God to choose if and when I could have my favorite dessert. I couldn't remember when anyone offered me cheesecake, so I assumed it would be a rare event.

The next afternoon, Friday, I walked down the street to where my daughter was playing at her friend's house. I asked the other mom how my daughter was doing. "Fine," she said. "Would you like to stay for a while? Yesterday was my birthday and I have some leftover cheesecake. Would you like a piece?"

I accepted, seeing this as God's sense of humor, allowing me to have my favorite dessert before the hard work of weight loose began. I imagined it would be a very long time before someone offered me cheesecake again.

The following day, Saturday, my other daughter spent the entire day at her friend's house. At the end of the day before dinner I drove there to pick her up. The other mom answered the door and invited me in. "Do you have time to stay for a while," she asked, "and spoil your dinner with a piece of cheesecake?" I didn't know what to think about her wonderful offer, but I accepted. It's cheesecake!

Sunday someone at home volunteered to go the market for a few things. When they returned an announcement was shouted from the kitchen, "We haven't had cheesecake for a very long time, so I bought one. Would anyone like a slice?"

I've learned more from other's view of this story than I can contemplate myself. My favorite explanation being, "Maybe God was trying to make you sick of it." But that's not possible and He knows it.

I think He was revealing His sense of humor and telling me He heard my prayer. Maybe He isn't concerned with my weight. I really don't know. But one thing I do know for sure, He loves you and me very much. It's His desire to reveal His existence to us. He is good and blesses us beyond what we deserve.

"Oh, taste and see that the LORD is good;
Blessed is the man who trusts in Him!"
Psalm 34:8

DIVINE DELAY

God directs our path

We didn't get very far. Our plans were halted when our tire went flat on the freeway. I was on my way to the beach with my family for a weekend getaway.

We exited the freeway and stopped on the shoulder of the off-ramp. AAA was called for assistance. The tow truck driver called to say he would be longer than the expected as he was still helping another driver. We decided to wait at the mini mart gas station across the street.

While we waited, a car stalled in the street on a slight incline. The driver quickly got out of his car while it was still in motion and tried to push it uphill but was losing momentum. He was trying to reach the intersection to make a U-turn around the center divider before turning into the gas station. There were others who could have helped him, but no one did, so I asked my children, "Should we watch him suffer or go help him push?" Together we ran into the street to push him around the corner. He was then able to coast the rest of the way into the station. We knew how he felt; we were in the same situation.

When the tow truck driver arrived, he was unable to change the tire. The wheel was fused on by weather. He would need to tow our car to a tire shop that had more powerful equipment. He put the car on his flatbed truck then told my young son and me to ride in the cab with him. The rest of my family would need to ride in our car on the flatbed.

Sitting inside the cab I noticed the tow truck driver's knuckles were extremely scabbed over on both hands. My son noticed them, too, and gave me an inquisitive look. After we were on the road I asked the driver what happened to his knuckles. He said I didn't want to know. I could tell my son wanted to know, and I had a pretty good idea after his remark.

It was becoming more obvious God had taken control over the events of our day and I believed it was no accident we were in his truck. I had a strange feeling he needed something we could help him with, which was weird because he was helping us. I told the driver I was honestly concerned about his welfare and I did want to know what happened to his knuckles.

His next question surprised me. He asked, "You aren't Christians, are you?" I could tell from his tone he was hoping we weren't. It was as if he wanted to avoid being judged.

My son didn't pick up the tone. He leaned forward to look at him. Wide-eyed he blurted out a happy, "Yes! We are!"

"Never mind," he told us. "I don't want to hear it. I grew up a Mormon and I know what you're going to say."

I assured him I wasn't a Mormon and we weren't typical Christians, that I was more concerned for him than his knuckles.

"OK," he said, "I got in a fight defending someone who was being attacked. I know Christians aren't supposed to fight, but I just couldn't stand by and watch what was happening, so I stopped it. I haven't told my parents yet because they'll really lay into me about it."

I explained to him that while God doesn't want us to start a fight, it's a whole other principle to protect someone from harm if we can. I told him the God of the Bible didn't want that person to be harmed. It was possible he was sent in response to that person's cry for help.

The driver seemed more at ease and said he hoped his parents would respond in the same way when they found out. I suggested he tell them the story from that perspective and they may understand.

Our slight detour taught me to see unexpected events differently. Though the day didn't go as I had planned, God had other plans for us. If the tire had not gone flat, the guy with the stalled car may not have been helped. Who knows, maybe in his time of need he cried out for help just before we saw him. If the tow truck driver was able to change the tire we wouldn't have been able to converse with him. Who knows, maybe he was asking God for courage to tell his parents what happened.

When we surrender every moment to the will of God, we will have a more glorious day when He is in control of it. When He stops you in your tracks, look around. Maybe you will find yourself being used as the hands, feet, and voice of God in another person's life that is seeking help.

"The steps of a good man are ordered by the Lord,
And He delights in his way."
Psalm 37:23

SUNDAY SCHOOL VISITOR
God's silent instruction

Third and fourth graders are engaging and eager to learn. It was always fun teaching them at Sunday School. The curriculum my church provided focused on main characters in the Bible such as Noah, Abraham, David and Goliath. Two sub-sections taught about God's creation and how to share one's faith with others.

To prepare for the class, I studied the Bible text and curriculum a little bit each day, finishing on Friday. Throughout the week I prayed for specific direction on what God wanted me to teach. Many of the students were from Christian families and repeatedly heard the same Bible stories. I sought God's guidance for truths that may be new to them in each story. God was always faithful to bless my time by revealing what He wanted me to teach.

However, one week God gave no guidance. After reading the lesson on Monday I felt no direction from the Lord. Each day of the week was the same. I had become used to the Holy Spirit guiding me, but when He remained quiet I became worried. I read the lesson again on Saturday and Sunday morning, but I felt empty without anything specific to teach the class. Frustrated at feeling unprepared, I said to God while driving to church, "OK God, you've given me nothing specific to teach, so I give this time to You. Maybe You have something else planned."

When all the children filed into the classroom I noticed we had a visitor. Two brothers brought a neighborhood friend with them. The visitor began asking questions about Jesus. Then he questioned the creation story that contradicted with the science books at his school.

The Lord then broke His silence with me. He spoke to my heart and mind with, "The students have been learning how to share their faith. Let them tell the new visitor what they know." And, "The class learned about My creation, let them tell the story."

After each visitor's question I asked the students to answer him, which they gladly did. The entire class time was spent with the visitor asking questions and the students explaining what they learned in the Bible. The scheduled lesson plan wasn't needed. What was needed was to answer a searching boy's questions. I sat back and marveled at God's glorious wisdom.

When the visitor ran out of questions the Lord instructed me again with, "Ask him if he wants to receive Jesus as his Savior." To my surprise, he was eager and willing. The students and I prayed with him, leading him in a prayer to receive Jesus as his Lord and Savior. Joy filled this new visitor's face and his whole countenance changed. The students were filled with a new enthusiasm for God and His Word. God's plan for the class far exceeded the lesson plan in a children's curriculum book. Our new visitor learned about Jesus and the students gained boldness in witnessing to others. I learned that being yielded to the Holy Spirit produces a greater outcome.

That day changed all of us for the better except the pastor's wife. She was scheduled to teach the class the following four Sundays after me. As I didn't teach the scheduled curriculum she became agitated. She was more concerned about how to follow with her scheduled lesson plan since I skipped mine. I told her God had a better lesson plan where He led a child to make a decision to follow Christ. Yet that didn't stop her from being disappointed with me for messing up her plans. I asked if the church had an extra Bible for this new student, but she ignored my question, still mumbling about how I didn't do my job.

The next week I brought the new student a Bible. He continued to come to church when he could get a ride from the brothers' family.

But that's not the end of the story.

We hadn't seen our new visitor at church for a long while. After the brothers' family moved to a different town, the visitor and his mom also moved, and they lost touch with each other. The brothers' mom asked if I had seen their young friend around town. I told her I saw him helping at the local farmer's market. He seemed very happy, but because he was working at one of the booths we weren't able to talk at the time. I suggested we pray and ask God to allow us to cross paths with him, which we did.

Three days later there was knock on my front door. It was the Sunday school visitor. I was so surprised to see him at my house because I didn't think he knew where I lived. He said he wasn't sure I lived there but saw a car in the driveway that looked like mine. He said the house looked happy like a Christian might live there, so he took a chance and knocked on the door. He was in the neighborhood visiting with other kids his age.

I told him we just prayed for him the previous Sunday hoping God would cause us to cross paths with him. I was amazed to see him so soon, especially at my front door. He didn't seem surprised by this at all, like this experience was normal for him. He said he still believed in Jesus, loving Him more than ever, and going to a church close to his new house. He said when I saw him at the farmer's market he was working for someone from his church. The work he was offered helped him and his mom with extra income. I was thrilled to hear how well God was taking care of him. I occasionally saw him around town. He was always happy and filled with enthusiastic joy.

"But Jesus said, 'Let the little children come to Me,
and do not forbid them; for of such is the kingdom of heaven.'"
Matthew 19:14

ELDERS
God's stories encourage others

I was criticized the previous week for witnessing to the Jehovah Witnesses who came to our house. I was told I was no longer allowed to speak with them. I ignored these snide remarks knowing God's approval of me was higher than that of the complainer.

The following week God set in motion new visitors. Two Mormon Elders walked up the driveway onto our porch. From the garage, I heard a sarcastic shout into the house, "Hey Kim! A couple of your friends are here to see you!"

Seeing the two young men at the front door made me think of a movie I saw called "The Other Side of Heaven." It was about a missionary who went to the Isle of Tonga. One of the young men standing at my door looked Polynesian and introduced himself as Elder Vakapuna. I asked him, "By any chance are you from the Isle of Tonga?"

"Why yes!" he said surprised. "How did you know?" I told him about the movie I saw and took a wild guess. He wasn't aware of the movie.

Elder Vakapuna and the other young man came to visit me very two weeks. When Elder Vakapuna was assigned to a different area, another young man was assigned in his place. Then those two came to my house every other week. The rotation continued that way for over a year.

When the young men arrived at my house they played foosball on my game table while I got them a glass of water. We visited for about an hour. They told me about their daily routine. Every morning they read the Book of Mormon for an hour, then ate breakfast before going door-to-door teaching others about their faith. I usually asked what God was personally teaching each of them. In turn, I shared what God was teaching me. I simply wanted to convey God's desire to have a personal relationship with them.

I typically asked them, "How have you seen God at work in your lives?"

To which they would reply, "We read the Book of Mormon and know it's true."

I rephrased my question with, "When have you seen God do something amazing that you clearly knew it was Him doing it? Something that was out of your control?"

"Like what?" they asked.

I then shared a God story like the time I tested a verse in Proverbs that says, *"A gift in secret subdues anger."* It's the seventh story in this book about a time when God subdued my boss's anger when I secretly gave him a roll of LifeSavers. The Elders had never heard of anyone applying the Bible's teaching in a given situation and then see a positive result.

The next time they came to visit they told me how amazed they were by what God did for my boss. In turn, they told their host family about the event. To find the verse in Proverbs, they read the entire book looking for it. They concluded with, "Wow, Proverbs is an amazing book!"

Each time the Elders visited I told them of the wondrous things God had done in my life and in the lives of others. At the end of that time, Elder Vakapuna revisited me. He had finished his two-year training in Southern California and wanted say goodbye to me before he left. What a joy that was for me. He shared how I had made an impression on him and all the others who came to my house. I felt like he and the other boys talked about their visits, though he didn't exactly say so and I didn't ask.

This experience taught me the value of sharing what God does in our lives, including those of different faiths. It's fruitless to compare Bible translations or books, where each person becomes defensive of their own. What can never be disputed are the many ways God reveals Himself to us. They are His stories, and they are meant to be shared because they point others to Him.

I don't know how those stories influenced each young man that came to my house, or what this story may be saying to you. But this I do know, as long as God opens a door for me to share His greatness with others, no amount of criticism is going to hinder me. There is nothing better in the history of the entire world than sharing the goodness of the Creator who made us. Who made you.

He is an awesome God and Father who loves you beyond all comprehension. He made you for His good pleasure to give you a future and a hope. The new life He offers you is free through the redemptive work of His Son Jesus Christ. All you need to do is believe He did this for you, repent of your sins and follow Him. Then He gives you His Holy Spirit to help you and teach you all things pertaining to this wonderful life. Oh, how He loves you!

"For God so loved the world
that He gave His only begotten Son,
that whosoever believes in Him shall not perish
but have everlasting life."
John 3:16

HOT WHEELS

God steers us in the right direction

I was on my way to visit a friend, but first I needed to stop at the store. While I was there I went into the toy aisle. I thought of purchasing toy trucks for my friend's boys to play with to occupy them while we visited.

Thinking my generosity would be pleasing to God I first looked at the large toy trucks. While I was deciding which ones to buy, an overwhelming conviction came over me. It felt like I shouldn't buy anything for the boys. When I didn't heed the conviction, my heart started to beat faster. The longer I stood there deciding which large toy trucks to buy the more convicted I got. The conviction became so intense I had to take my sweater off as I was physically heating up.

My intentions seemed honorable, but the Holy Spirit was telling me something different. Still not completely listening, I thought the Holy Spirit might be telling me the larger trucks were too excessive. I made a selection of three $1 Hot Wheels cars thinking God wouldn't object to the small gifts.

With the three tiny cars tucked in my purse I went to meet my friend. I planned to give the cars to her boys as my friend and I sat down for a chat. It wasn't until I arrived that God made it clear why the gifts were inappropriate. The boys weren't allowed to play for some trouble they got themselves into. Purchasing the big toy trucks would have been a waste. The three small Hot Wheels remained in my purse.

Has this ever happened to you? Have you ever felt like God was speaking to you with words you can't hear? It's hard to comprehend at the time. If you're a believer in God the Father, a follower of Jesus, and yielded to the Holy Spirit, He's going to lead you in a fruitful and beneficial life. More importantly, He's going to perpetually reveal Himself to you through your normal circumstances.

God uses moments like this to teach us to better hear His voice. It's not an audible voice, but a thought, a strong feeling, a conviction, or a nudge. It's usually moments or days later when we learn why His still, small voice was instructing us. God wants to guide us in every aspect of our lives, in a way that leads to blessing and life and joy. Ultimately, He is leading us to Himself.

"For the LORD gives wisdom;
From His mouth come knowledge and understanding;
He stores up sound wisdom for the upright;
He is a shield to those who walk uprightly;
He guards the paths of justice,
And preserves the way of His saints.
Then you will understand righteousness and justice,
Equity and every good path."
Proverbs 2:6-9

THE ELEVENTH HOUR

God is ever-present

It was a Wednesday night, March 2009. Exhausted I went to bed early about eight o'clock. Later that night a troubling feeling jolted me out of sleep. Wide-awake, I looked at the time on my digital clock. It read 11:11*pm.

Thinking the rest of my family was home asleep I got out of bed and walked downstairs to turn off a light that had been left on. I sat at the kitchen table drinking a glass of water wondering why I was awake and feeling troubled.

I went back to bed, but I lay there unable to go back to sleep. A nagging feeling overcame me to pray for the safety of my children, a daughter in particular. I thought this was odd because I believed my children were all home in bed. I prayed anyway, for their safety and protection against whatever may want to harm them. I then felt the Holy Spirit lead me to go back downstairs. I assumed He wanted me to pray in another room. It was 11:48 pm.

When I reached the bottom of the stairs in the entry hall, someone was outside trying to unlock the front door. Startled that someone was trying to break in confirmed the need for prayer. Instead, it was my 21-year-old daughter coming inside. We were both surprised, not expecting to see the other.

She had been visiting a friend in San Diego, then wanted to know why I was up standing at the front door. I told her I was suddenly woken at 11:11, urged to pray, then prompted to walk downstairs again where we met at the door.

"That's weird," she said. "Just as I got in the car to drive home I checked the clock on the dashboard. It said 11:11."

Dear reader, when we yield to God's call, moments like these become very precious. God allows us to participate in His plans and reveal He is at work in our lives and in the lives of others. This time the call was to pray for the protection of a child and see her safely return home.

"But as for me, I trusted in You, O LORD.
I say You are my God. My times are in Your hand;"
Psalm 30:14-15a

*For those concerned about the number 11:11 being associated with occult practices, I have been made aware of that. However, in this case I had nothing to do with when I woke up, or when my daughter entered her car. God could have used any time, but He chose that time. Granted, each of our clocks could have been off by a few minutes, but that's not the point, for God was fully aware of that, too. The enemy has infiltrated all aspects of God's creation in an effort to distort it. God is the One who created time when He created the sun, moon, and stars. God also created this event to remind my daughter and me that He is the One who is in control of time, events, and circumstances. It was God who woke me to pray for the safety of my daughter. It just happened to be eleven minutes after 11pm when He did so.

BROTHER'S CALL
God frustrates schemers

There's a note in the margin of my Bible that reads, "Brother's call, April 12, 2010." I was seeking God for answers on how to deal with a hurtful, manipulative person. As I prayed and searched the Bible for answers my phone rang. My brother, who lived 1000 miles away, called to give me a Bible verse. He didn't know what the verse said; he only had the book, chapter, and verse.

He said, "I'm driving with my wife and I received a Bible verse I think the Lord wants me to tell you. Do you have a pencil? Good, write this down: Job 5:8. Got it? OK. Bye!"

My brother didn't know the situation I was in, yet God used him to answer my prayer. I read through to verse 16. The text reads,

> "But as for me, I would seek God, and to God I would commit my cause— Who does great things, and unsearchable, marvelous things without number. He gives rain on the earth, and sends waters on the fields. He sets on high those who are lowly, and those who mourn are lifted to safety. He frustrates the devices of the crafty, so that their hands cannot carry out their plans. He catches the wise in their own craftiness, and the counsel of the cunning comes quickly upon them. They meet with darkness in the daytime, and grope at noontime as in the night. But He saves the needy from the sword, from the mouth of the mighty, and from their hand. So the poor have hope, and injustice shuts her mouth."

God used these verses to remind me to commit my cause to Him. I didn't need to worry, but trust that God was able to frustrate the devices of the crafty person so that they could not carry out their devious plan. No harm ever came to me. Instead, God renewed my hope in Him and proved He does great and marvelous things for those who seek Him.

DIARRHEA DUDE
God thwarts the plans of the wicked

When I think of God thwarting a wicked person's plans, Haman in the book of Ruth comes to mind. I trust God's ability to do this based on the biblical story. I am personally aware of times when God kept me safe, like when I was man-handled in Mazatlán in the eleventh story of this book. However, I never learned the details of how God actually thwarted anyone in my lifetime until this event.

A person working in my office volunteered to manage my business under the premise I was overburdened with it. By relinquishing some of my responsibilities, I would have more time to create. This sounded good to me. However, he was not responsible. Instead, he stopped paying the bills, refused to disclose how money was being spent, and squandered it on selfish pursuits.

My office staff pulled me aside and told me the full scope of the negligence. I knew something had to be done, but there was reason for me to be cautious. This person, who masqueraded as a thoughtful Christian, proved otherwise. Instead, his actions were exploitative. I didn't know what else he was capable of doing once he discovered he no longer had the control he manipulated for. To avoid an explosive confrontation, I felt I needed to proceed stealthily.

I began with a prayer, "Oh Lord God, this is Your business. You created it and bless it. I know you don't want it mismanaged, squandered, or misrepresented. Please help me right the wrongs."

I asked my staff to help me on a morning he would be out of the office at an event. We worked quickly opening new accounts, transferring information, and closing old accounts. The process took longer than anticipated validating new information and waiting for confirmation. We were sweating, literally.

Then a call came in from the culprit. He said he would be out of the office longer than planned with the excuse he needed to rush home to take care of an issue. When asked what the issue was he said he had to change his pants, as there must have been something he ate that didn't agree with him.

He called again a short time later. He said he tried to return to his event but was repeatedly afflicted with whatever it was he ate. He was returning home to shower and change clothes again. After cleaning up, he called a third time. He said he wouldn't make it to the office that day and apologized for the inconvenience. I reassured him that everything was under control in the office and he wasn't needed there. By midafternoon all the transfers were complete, and the unaccountable manipulator had been kept away with issues out of his control.

A few days later when the new account statements arrived in the mail I was confronted about the changed accounts, but by this time there was nothing diarrhea dude could do about it. In retaliation, he initiated a hurtful scheme that became evident a few years later, but God took care of that, also.

"He frustrates the devices and schemes of the crafty,
So that their hands cannot attain success or
achieve anything of [lasting] worth.
He catches the [so-called] wise in their own shrewdness,
And the advice of the devious is quickly thwarted."
Job 5:12-13 AMP

SORE LOSER
God does not forsake His own

This is one of my favorite stories, not because of the circumstances, for they were dreadful. But because God honored what seemed like a ridiculous prayer. It was in the fall of 2010, I was still married to my ex-husband who was displaying some unusual behavior. He was aloof, gone for long periods of time, and pushing me away relationally with his demeaning words. I suspected he was up to something, but I didn't know exactly what. So, I prayed to the One who did know.

My prayer was influenced by my current study of the Israelites' freedom from Egypt. I asked the all-knowing, all-powerful God, "If my husband is doing something he isn't supposed to be doing, something that is harmful to me, make it clear to me by making him break out in sores on his body. But, Lord, only if You want to. I know this is a ridiculous prayer, and I'm sorry if it's inappropriate. Amen."

I can guess what you might be thinking based on the responses I've received from others I shared this story with. Some have looked at me like I'm the boy in the Twilight Zone episode who wishes people into the cornfield. I need to tell you, I have no super powers, I cannot make anything happen by praying for it, and I wish no one any harm. My reason for making such a bold prayer was due to my isolation from others my ex-husband created. I had no other resource for help and his abuses were escalating.

The day after my prayer my husband was holding a damp warm washcloth over his left eye that was now red and inflamed. I wondered if this was a coincidence or the answer to my prayer because he had suffered something similar in the past. Two days later his right cheek was bright red from an obvious rash. I had never seen that before. Later that week his left shin had a raised round sore just above his white calf sock that he was worried about.

God had my attention. It looked like He was answering my ridiculous prayer. It seemed clear God was confirming that my husband was up to something he shouldn't be doing. My suspicions seemed validated that his actions, whatever they were, could potentially harm me.

With three ailments at once, my husband was nervously pacing in and out of the kitchen door and onto the patio, then into the garage. I was watching him from the kitchen table and pondering the situation. I got up to ask him the question I already knew the answer to. Standing in the kitchen doorway I asked him, "What's with all the sores on your body?" Standing in the middle of the patio, without looking at me, he said he had no idea. I told him, "I think I know why."

His gaze was now intense, and he angrily waited for me to explain. I revealed my earlier prayer asking God to show me if he was doing something he shouldn't be doing by making him break out in sores on his body. I half expected him, who claimed to be a Christian, to be somewhat remorseful and repent, seeing the mighty hand of God manifested by the three sores on his body. Instead, he was furious. He asked why I would pray such a ridiculous prayer, as though he believed God had answered it by afflicting him.

The moment was intense, amusing, and tragic all at the same time. It was intense because I didn't know how far he would express his anger. It was humorous seeing how God actually answered my prayer. In our marriage my husband typically had the upper hand and now God's hand was upon him. It was also heartbreaking seeing him exposed for doing something he shouldn't be doing without any remorse.

In response to his question of why I would pray such a ridiculous prayer, I replied, "The real question is: what are you doing that you shouldn't be doing?" With an indignant grunt, he walked away from me into the garage without an answer.

I had never prayed a prayer like this before, and I had no idea what the outcome of that prayer would be. I knew something wasn't right, but I had no way of knowing for sure. I believe God's answer to my prayer wasn't meant to harm my ex. He eventually recovered from his sores. For him, I believe this event was a wake-up call from God that he never heeded. For me, God's answer was a merciful and kind validation of my suspicions by showing me I had real cause for concern.

"For the Lord loves justice and does not forsake His godly ones;
they are preserved forever,
but the descendants of the wicked will be cut off."
Psalm 37:28

TAKING FLIGHT

God renews our strength

There are moments in life when despair becomes overwhelming. On this day it was very early in the morning on Good Friday. I left for a drive along the coast from Carlsbad to Encinitas to escape the chaos at home.

Traveling south on Pacific Coast Highway along the shore, a flock of twenty-two pelicans flew to the right of me. They glided over the ocean keeping perfect pace with the speed of my car. They kept me company traveling in the same direction for miles. It was as if the Lord sent them there to cheer me up, and it was working. I took delight in watching them glide beside me. I was the only car on the road, and all the traffic lights remained green in my favor.

Ahead, the road veered away from the beach where a bluff rose above the shore. I imagined I would soon lose sight of the flock. They sped up ahead of me as they gained height towards the top of the hill. Just as they reached the edge of the cliff, instead of landing as I suspected, they veered right to soar out over the ocean. As they did, more pelicans launched off the top of the hill to follow them like ribbons over the sea. Their numbers were innumerable. I parked my car and got out as more pelicans continued to fly out over the sea to join the others.

It was an overcast day and the sea was unusually calm. I had lived at the coast for over ten years, passed this location many times, yet never saw or experienced this before. I was overwhelmed by the display God provided for my enjoyment. He was being a loving Father taking away the pain of my circumstances. He was telling me I was not alone, that He sees me.

The chaos that ensued previously that morning paled in comparison to this spectacular event I was now witnessing. My spirit lifted in wonder at the mighty hand of God over His creation.

"I will lift You up, O Lord, for You have lifted me up.
You have not let those who hate me stand over me in joy."
Psalm 30:1

"But those who trust in the Lord will find new strength.
They will soar high on wings like eagles.
They will run and not grow weary;
they will walk and not faint."
Isaiah 40:31

BALBOA PARK
God cares about little things

I didn't care if I looked ridiculous. Overjoyed, I crossed the street into the center median to photograph what God had done. No one can convince me He isn't concerned about small matters.

It was Christmas time and we were trying to find a parking space at Balboa Park's Festival of Lights in San Diego. Not believing it would be crowded we arrived as it opened. We were wrong about the crowds. All the parking lots were full, and the street was lined with cars for miles.

After driving through all the parking lots and down the road without finding a place to park, I turned around and headed back toward the freeway. Out loud I prayed, "God if you want us to go to this festival, please open up a place for us to park. Otherwise, we'll head back home."

Slowly I drove past the gazillion parked cars searching for an open parking space. Just as we arrived at the front of the park a car pulled out from the curb leaving an available space. There is no way we could have been any closer. It was the closest place to park to the entrance, even closer than in a parking lot.

Though this is only a little story, nothing God does is small. He is always creating ways to delight us and let us know He cares. Everything He does has significance, even if it's only to provide a parking space. The next time you need a place to park your car, ask God. He is able to provide one.

"The works of the LORD are great,
Studied by all who have pleasure in them."
Psalm 111:2

THROUGH THE WATERS

God is our shelter

The previous weeks were spent in much prayer and Bible study. I was seeking the Lord for direction on what to do about a stressful situation. That part of the story is irrelevant. What needs to be emphasized is the path God led me on, or rather, through. It was late February 2011.

My prayer time and Bible studies repeatedly led to the same or similar scripture verses. The Holy Spirit spoke to me through scripture that contained instructions to leave, which was sad, because I didn't want to leave. As the week progressed the conviction to leave grew stronger, and the verses God opened up to me became more specific.

A verse on Monday spoke of traveling in five days. For me that pointed to Saturday. I didn't think it was significant until I read a verse on Wednesday that spoke of leaving in three days, also Saturday. Each time I read those verses I felt the Holy Spirit instructing me to pay attention to the text. I wasn't looking for any specific scripture verses. I was simply asking God what He wanted me to do. It felt like He was shouting at me.

There was only one place I could go, a small vacation house in Northern California. To get there I had to drive over the Tejon Pass. A snowstorm was expected in the mountain range on Saturday morning. Loved ones advised me to postpone my trip until the weather cleared. Their advice was logical and normally I would have heeded their warning. However, to not leave on that Saturday felt like disobedience to the Holy Spirit's direction. In other words, fear of grieving the Holy Spirit was stronger than my fear of driving through a snowstorm over a mountain pass. I packed the car on Friday and watched weather reports throughout the night. The snowstorm was imminent. Weather cameras through the pass became iced over making it impossible to see the highway.

I didn't understand why God asked me to do this hard thing. Yet early Saturday morning I began the 500-mile drive north from Carlsbad, faithfully believing I was doing what He instructed me to do. I was nervous and unsure I even heard Him correctly.

As I started the car a friend called to ask if I'd stop at her house before I left town. There we prayed for God's continued guidance and protection. She gave me a music CD of instrumental worship and Bible readings. With many tears, we said good-bye. I had no idea how long I would be gone. I was simply letting myself be led by the Holy Spirit to discover what God wanted to teach me. I was going to be alone with God; I needed to hear Him. I needed to know His will.

On the highway I put the CD in. I had never heard it before. The music was soothing, and the readings were uplifting. Driving north, clouds began to blow in from the west. There wasn't any rain until I reached Los Angeles. Then it was only a light rain that lasted for five minutes. After that, a clear patch of blue sky opened up above me.

At the base of the mountains ahead of me, thick clouds came into view whose heights were taller than the mountain range. I already knew the steepness of the pass; I'd driven this route many times before. This was the first time I saw clouds larger than the height of the mountain. I remember taking in a deep breath at the ominous view. This Southern California girl had no experience driving in snow; it didn't look good.

As I became fearful of the storm ahead, the next song began to play. After a long instrumental beginning, a woman's voice sang the lyrics, "I will take you through the waters...." I had no doubt those timely lyrics were God's immediate comfort. I remember nervously saying to God out loud, "OK, here we go!" If He was truly guiding me north, I trusted Him to get me there safely.

As for the clear patch of blue sky that opened up above me after leaving Los Angeles, it was still with me. I had sunshine overhead and a dry road below. Beyond the patch of clear blue sky, gray clouds stretched to the horizon.

I stopped for lunch at the foothills before making the steepest climb through the Tejon Pass. Inside the restaurant, a group of potato farmers from Idaho were in line ahead of me. They were traveling south to a potato convention. This may not be funny to you, but it was to me at the time. I wondered why there was a potato convention in Southern California instead of in Idaho where most potatoes are grown. I wondered if God orchestrated this meeting to bring me relief from the stress I was experiencing. The farmers had driven south through the pass and reported the beginning of snow, but the roads were open. They were surprised to see the sun shining overhead and the ground dry. I joked with them that the patch of blue sky was traveling north with me, though I wasn't really sure.

When I left the restaurant the patch of blue sky overhead did continued to follow me up the mountain to Fort Tejon. I stopped at the Fort to marvel at the beauty of the white snow on the hills contrasted with the dark leafless trees in the distance. The sunshine made the snow sparkle and melt in drops you could hear fall from the trees. It was lovely, and I was blessed to witness it, honored to be in that spot at that exact time. It felt like something holy was happening.

The only other sound was of a young family playing in the snow. They were from the valley on the other side of the mountain.

One other car was parked at the Fort. A couple had also driven over the pass from the north. They asked me about the road conditions further south. They were surprised to see snow all around with clear blue sky above. I told them I couldn't predict the weather behind me, as I had only seen blue sky and dry ground, claiming the patch of blue sky overhead was following me. They thought I was joking, and to be honest, I was trying to comprehend the thought of it myself.

For the remainder of my journey the patch of blue sky followed me overhead for 500 miles. It was confirmation that I was in the Lord's care, exactly where He wanted me to be. Other drivers along the way reported rough weather and heavy downpours. I traveled on dry roads and never used my windshield wipers again after the sprinkle in Los Angeles.

"When you pass through the waters,
I will be with you;
And through the rivers,
they shall not overflow you."
Isaiah 43:2

SURPRISE FIND

God's word is a treasure

While studying God's word in a small town without internet or TV, I was wishing I had a larger word concordance than the one in the back of my Bible. There were several topics I wanted to study further. I also wanted to know the root meanings of words that were translated differently in the various Bible versions I had with me.

I walked into town for some ice cream and discovered an advertisement in the local paper announcing a book sale at the neighborhood library. Curious, I went to see what they had. Being a small library, I expected to find novels and worn out children's books. A sign on the entry door read, "SALE! All books $1.00." Arrows led to a small room in the back.

On the top of a tall shelf against the back wall, a thick bright green hardback caught my eye. I reached up and brought it down to see what kind of book it was. "That book is going to cost you $2.00," came a shout from a woman sitting at an old wooden desk. "It's too big to let go for just $1.00."

I nodded at her and redirected my attention to the book. The gold lettering on the cover read, "STRONG'S EXHAUSTIVE CONCORDANCE OF THE BIBLE." It looked brand new, like it had never been opened. The edges of the pages were also tinted green to match the cover. The pages showed no wear and appeared to have never been opened, as they were still stuck together from when the tint was added.

I happily gave the woman $2.00 and saw the book as a gift from God. With it He continued to speak to me His words that I needed to hear.

"I rejoice at Your word,
As one who finds a great treasure."
Psalm 119:162

BIG DIPPER

God is always near

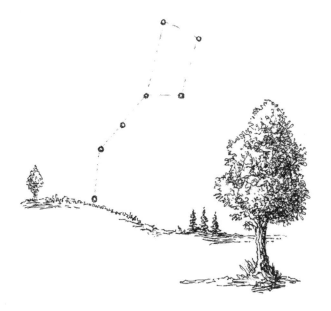

I was staying at a friend's house because it was no longer safe for me to be in my home. The hostility that escalated at home caused me to suspect it might stalk me. So, when the Lord woke me at 4am, instructing me to look outside, I naturally assumed I was being warned of a danger lurking there.

I peeked through the shutters into the dark morning but there was nothing to be afraid of. Instead, the Big Dipper constellation was low on the horizon looking larger than normal. I had never seen it in that position before. The scoop of the Dipper was at the top with its handle arching downward. The end of the handle appeared to be resting on the horizon.

I grabbed my sketchpad and quickly doodled the scene in the dark. By the time I was finished sketching I could no longer see the Big Dipper. The sun began to rise, and the early morning light turned the sky a light dusty blue hue. I was overwhelmed by God's kindness to wake me in time to see the spectacular sight before it disappeared.

That small encounter filled me with joy in a troublesome time. Even though the light quickly dispelled the darkness and hid the Dipper from view I knew it was still there. God used His creation to remind me that He was still with me even though I couldn't see Him. He also comforted me by demonstrating His authority over His creation. Light always dispels the darkness and drives it away. In the same way the rising sun drove away the darkness of the night sky, so too God has the ultimate power over the darkness in other realms.

"Then I saw that wisdom excels folly,
As light excels darkness."
Ecclesiastes 2:13

"But you are a chosen generation,
a royal priesthood, a holy nation, His own special people,
that you may proclaim the praises of Him who called you
out of darkness into His marvelous light;"
1 Peter 2:9

AS THE LORD LEADS
God guides

I was in a state of limbo, staying somewhere temporarily. Wondering where the Lord would lead me was always on my mind. I longed to be where God could use me. I also wanted to be someplace safe and free to be the person God created me to be. I imagined many different scenarios while being open to the Holy Spirit's leading. Unbeknownst to me at the time, God began opening the doors that would lead me to where I am now.

A door first cracked opened on Friday, November 18, 2011, as I sat waiting in the San Diego airport. I was on my way to visit my brother and his family for the week of Thanksgiving. With a new sketchbook in hand, I contemplated what to draw on the first page. I was on my way to Oregon, so I wrote, "O R E G O N" across the top. It had been a long time since I was there so below I wrote, "A NEW STATE." I studied the words deciding how to complete this drawing. Then it came to me, "A new state OF MIND," like a pun. Under the words I sketched a little cottage with trees and a garden.

The Lord began speaking to me through my illustration. I held back tears not wanting anyone see me cry. I began grieving as the Lord clearly said, "I'm leading you to Oregon."

I remember thinking, "I haven't even left the San Diego airport and You're already speaking to me about Oregon." Moving to Oregon never occurred to me. It was much farther than I imagined moving. It was too far away from my children.

That week visiting my brother's family in Oregon was spectacular. I was on visual overload from the autumn trees covered in yellow, orange, red and fuchsia leaves. I was emotionally and spiritually renewed as my brother and his family made me laugh, took me on adventures, and shared their faith. It was like having church every day, my soul fully fed and nourished. Leaving them was difficult. The image of my sister-in-law crying from the passenger seat of their car, as they dropped me off at the airport and drove away, has never left me. Though I didn't see it at the time, a door had inched open.

It wouldn't be until March of 2012 when I was able to actually move. With no specific place to go, I planned to put my belongings in storage and take another trip to Oregon to be sure that's where God wanted me to be. My brother, a very logical man, said that was a ridiculous idea. If I truly believed God wanted me to move to Oregon, and I already had to pack my things in a moving truck, I should just do it once and drive everything north. He offered to find a storage facility near him and let me stay with his family until I found my own home. The love I felt from his family made the decision easier. Looking back, I can now see how God used my brother's words of wisdom to help me take the next step to where God was leading me.

To get pricing online for a moving truck I had to submit my e-mail address. The rest of my information I kept general, with no specific dates. I compared the different options and prices of each rental company, overwhelmed by the decision of actually renting a truck to haul everything to a different state. An email reply came from the owner of my local Penske Rental. They offered a reduced price for a larger truck that would be available for pick up in three days. I booked the rental seeing that as a sign from God. I needed to move in five days and estimated it would take two days to load my business and home items.

When I picked up the truck I discovered the owner was a woman. At no additional charge, she upgraded my car towing bar to a car trailer, stating it would be much easier for me to maneuver. One of her guys put my car on the trailer and hitch it to the truck. The truck was so tall I had to climb two steps up into the cab. I felt so inadequate driving such a large truck, but the woman behind the counter reassured me I'd be fine. She was confident I could do it. It's hard to explain, but I felt like she had some insight into my situation, like God was telling her to grant me favor. The door on my journey was widening and I was about to drive through it.

I'm not going to minimize the 1000-mile drive north. It was often brutal. Leaving at 4 am while it was still dark, I cried most of the morning. I was scared driving that loaded diesel beast by myself, and I was angry with the person who put me in this situation. With deep sorrow, I was grieving for moving so far away from my children. It was difficult trying to handle the huge steering wheel and see in the dark while wiping tears from my face.

Relief came later that morning when my mom joined me at the base of the Tejon Pass. That first mountain pass was a difficult climb. Most of the weight in the truck consisted of boxes of greeting cards and business supplies. I thought that once we got through the Tejon Pass in California it would be smooth sailing the rest of the way. I was wrong; the Siskiyou Pass in Oregon was worse. The big yellow beast maxed out at 20 mph up the steep hills as semitrucks passed us.

The only pleasant part about the drive was how pretty the scenery became the further north we traveled. When we arrived at my brother's home two days later, my sister-in-law looked up at me in the driver seat and said, "Now I know why 'berly' is in the middle of your name." I had made it this far. Next, I anticipated walking through the door of a home that God was leading me to.

I viewed several homes in the Salem area for a month without success. There were plenty of houses for sale, but none suited my needs or made me feel at home.

My sister-in-law's mom suggested three times, "Why don't you move to Mount Angel?" I didn't give her suggestion much thought, as I didn't know where Mount Angel was, nor did I know anyone there. The third time she suggested it we were on our way to see the tulip fields. She brought a clipping from the newspaper of a home for sale in Mount Angel, words only, no photo. She thought we could look at it since we would be driving through Mount Angel. When we arrived at the house I could see it was vacant. I remember thinking a strange thought, "If it has seven steps up to the porch, I'm getting it." It did.

I took down the information on the sign and enjoyed the rest of the day. Work was busy the following week in a makeshift office at my brother's home. I soon forgot about the Mount Angel house. A realtor in Salem added to my exhaustion by bombarding me with home listings that didn't interest me. The doors in Salem were closing.

I sat in my car in front of my brother's house. Frustrated I cried out to God, "Just dump something in my lap; I'm exhausted from looking at houses!" Immediately my cell phone rang. It was a different realtor my brother previously put me in contact with. He said he had a house in Silverton with a big porch that might suit my needs. Then I remember the Mount Angel house with its big porch. Mount Angel is next to Silverton. I told him about it and he called the sellers. The sellers happened to be at the house and could show it to me right away. I grabbed my ten-year-old nephew who knew the territory and we arrived within thirty minutes.

When I walked in the front door, I had a sensation like that of an arm waving me in. I know that sounds odd. It felt odd to me at the time. But with it was a *knowing* that I was supposed to be there, that this was the place I was being led to. I felt so sure that this home was from God that I almost told my realtor I'd take it after simply walking through the front door. Touring the rest of the home confirmed my feeling and revealed it was also perfect for my business. I told my realtor I'd take it, he suggested an offer, which was exactly what I could afford, and the owners accepted it.

The amazing part about acquiring this home is I didn't have anything to do with finding it. God used others and a series of circumstances to dump it into my lap. Once I saw it I knew it was the one. The door had fully opened, and God had shoved me through it.

To clarify, my heart's desire wasn't for a house or its location. My heart longed to be in God's will and be led where He wanted me to be. I was only trying to follow His lead, often wavering, but always searching, and He kept leading. My home is perfect for me and God knew it. It's in a small rural farming town; there isn't even a traffic light. The house is an old Craftsman that's in town, but off the beaten path, perfect walking distance from the Post Office and shops in town. I can see the main part of town and those driving through it from my office, which I enjoy. My neighbors are wonderful, and the porch is large. I have plenty of room to grow a garden, and ample space to live and work.

In the days and years that followed, God continued to reveal and confirm I'm where He wants me to be. Remember at the beginning of this story I told of my visit to Oregon the week of Thanksgiving? Through the children that grew up in this home, I learned their mom lived here for sixty years. The week I came to visit my brother, their mom went into the hospital and passed away at the age of eighty. The week God told me He was leading me to Oregon was the same week He took Mrs. Moyer to her eternal home. I now have the privilege of occupying her temporary residence here on earth.

In many ways, I've learned Mrs. Moyer and I have a lot in common: our love of God, our devotion time set aside to pray and learn from Him, our love of the color pink, and tea time. A large shelf in the kitchen now displays my collection of teacups. Like her, I enjoy walking to the post office and sitting on the front porch visiting with neighbors.

Once while visiting with friends in the neighborhood, discussing how long each of us had lived in Mount Angel, one friend told me, "It feels like you've always been here." Her kind words were another confirmation from God that I'm where He wants me to be because I'm the newest kid on the block.

It wasn't always easy getting here. I often wavered trying to understand what God wanted me to do. Yet He proved He was always in control. He was the One opening all the right doors ahead of me as I yielded my life to Him.

"I know your works. See, I have set before you an open door,
and no one can shut it; for you have a little strength,
have kept My word, and have not denied My name."
Revelation 3:8

A KNOCK AT THE DOOR

God removes loneliness

I just moved into my new home. Once the hard work of unboxing was at a stage where I felt settled, a deep sense of loneliness set in. I sat at the dining room table expressing my feelings to God when someone knocked on my door. I pulled myself together and wiped the tears from my face before answering it. I had no idea who it was. I wasn't expecting anyone, and I didn't know anyone in town.

It was a woman I never met before. She introduced herself as a friend of the previous owners. Her big smile was welcoming, and I invited her in.

It wasn't long before she asked, "Are you all right?"

"No. Just before you knocked on my door I was telling God how lonely I was."

"Ahhh, come here," she said. "You need a hug."

It was apparent God had a hand in orchestrating her timely visit, though I'm not sure she was aware of it at the time. Her kindness was comforting, and her visit reassured me that I wasn't really alone. Through her, God made His presence known.

Weeks later I asked what prodded her to come visit me at that specific time. She seemed reluctant to answer. Guessing the reason, I asked if she was curious to see who bought Mrs. Moyer's house. She smiled and admitted she was. We both laughed. She remains a dear friend to this day.

"In my distress I called upon the LORD,
And cried out to my God;
He heard my voice from His temple,
And my cry came before Him, even to His ears."
Psalm 18:6

KEY INSTRUCTION
Out of the mouth of babes

I hadn't been in Oregon very long and was still learning my way around. My ten-year-old nephew can beautifully navigate the area, so I often took him with me. His help typically included a stop for lunch at his place of choice.

After we stopped for lunch I couldn't start my car. The key went in the ignition, but it wouldn't rotate forward to start it. It was like something was hindering it from turning.

My nephew said, "Take the key out and turn it around."

"That's silly," I said. "The key is the same on both sides."

"Just try it, Aunt Kim."

Again, I told him, "That's ridiculous."

"Trust me, just do it!" he urged me.

"OK." What did I have to lose? I took the key out, turned it around, and put it back in the ignition. This time the key turned perfectly to start the car. Can you guess who had the biggest smile on his face?

It's true the Holy Spirit uses children to speak to us. This was a reminder for me to listen to the suggestion of others, even a ten-year-old. It's important to live in community with other believers because the Holy Spirit uses God's children of all ages to bless, encourage, and guide one another in life and wisdom.

"Out of the mouth of babes and nursing infants
You have ordained strength,"
Psalm 8:2a

ALEAH'S RASH
God Heals

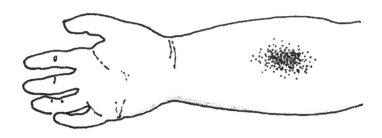

Aleah was five, a sweet blond-haired girl with bright eyes and a cheerful smile. She was one of three children from next door who came to visit me in the afternoon. We played games on my front porch: Go Fish, Old Maid, and Uno. The children often talked about their day at school, their conflicts with other kids, special events, and visits with relatives. I looked for opportunities to teach them about Jesus and the Bible.

One afternoon I noticed a small rash on the inside of Aleah's right arm. The next day it was bigger. The Lord urged me to ask if I could pray for her rash, to ask God if He would heal it. She covered the rash with her left hand and flat out refused. Her older sister, age seven, encouraged her to let me pray for her. She tried to tell Aleah that I was only going to ask God to make it better, but Aleah would not allow it.

The following day Aleah came by herself to visit. Her rash was bigger than before. After a game of Go Fish, I asked again if I could pray for her rash. She hesitated at first, but finally agreed to let me pray for her.

I cupped my hand over the rash on her arm and prayed, "Dear Lord, You love Aleah, and to prove to her that you love and care for her, please heal the rash on her arm. Amen."

I wasn't sure what to expect. I mainly wanted her to know God was real, that He loved and cared for her. When I took my hand off her arm we looked at each other and gasped.

Smiling, Aleah said in amazement, "Do you see that? It's smaller!"

"Yes, I do!" I was shocked myself. I told her God is amazing and loves her very much.

She ran off shouting, "I have to go show my mom!"

"O LORD my God,
I cried out to You,
And You healed me."
Psalm 30:2

JUPITER AND THE MOON
God's delights us

Have you ever gone out of your way to show something to someone you love? Something specific that will make them happy? It's similar to a parent showing a puppy to a child or taking a sweetheart to watch a beautiful sunset. It's that special moment your heart is delighted because someone dear to you is overjoyed. God does the same for us!

One night, I could have missed what God wanted to show me if He had answered my prayer. It was a simple prayer. I was exhausted and wanted to sleep. I went to bed early at 8:30pm. I typically sleep very well, but on December 20th, 2013 sleep escaped me. After a restless hour, I became frustrated and yelled out loud, "God, help me! I just want to go to sleep!"

A moment later a bright light from outside flooded my room. I climbed out of bed to discover a huge full moon brighter than I've ever seen before. I was surprised to see anything in the sky, it had been overcast all week. Next to the moon was a large bright star I later learned was Jupiter. Those in the Pacific Northwest could observe this event on that specific night when Jupiter would be at its closest to the moon in twenty-five years at 9:30 pm.

No longer tired, I put my coat over my pajamas and stood outside gazing at God's handiwork. Not only did He create the event I was admiring, but He kept me awake to see it, then cleared the sky of clouds in the middle of winter.

"The heavens declare the glory of God;
And the firmament shows His handiwork."
Psalm 19:1

FEAR NO MORE
God fights for us

I'm not going to lie to you. When you choose to follow Jesus, and be a vessel in His hand, you're going to be attacked. Satan's goal is to distract, deceive, and discourage people from following and believing in God. Satan often uses other people who are easily controlled by his power and influence as weapons against us. When you become wise to this tactic and are no longer affected by the distraction, deceit, or discouragement of others, he'll send one of his evil spirits to invade your thoughts.

One morning I woke early at 4:30am, completely rested. All was peaceful and quiet. I was enjoying listening to my cat move on the ironing board across the room. Suddenly a thought came into my mind accusing me of being a loser; ridiculing me for not accomplishing worldly pursuits as though I was lagging behind the masses. As a consequence, I would suffer from my own negligence. The thoughts were so strong I could no longer remain in bed.

After petting my cat, I went into the kitchen wondering where these thoughts came from. I questioned myself. Was I really a loser? What should I be doing that I'm not doing now? How will I suffer? Then I simply prayed, "Lord, what do you want me to do?"

His answer was surprising yet simple, "Turn on the radio."

That wasn't what I expected but I did it anyway. The lyrics of the first worship song were, "Come to my rescue, be lifted high." God used the words to reassure me that He was my rescuer and the thoughts were a spiritual attack. The titles of the next consecutive songs that played were, "Savior King," "I Belong to You," "Nothing Like Your Love," and "Good Good Father."

As I listened to each song God reminded me that He is my Savior, I am His, He loves me, and He is a good Father who is perfect in all His ways to us. My anxiety diminished, and my spirit lifted, as the Lord cast out the enemy's deceptive words and replaced them with His truth and joy. I started journaling this experience while the worship music continued to play in the background. Overwhelmed by God's loving Spirit that flooded my home, I was moved to tears. I stopped journaling and simply rested in God's sweet loving presence.

God doesn't expect us to live as the world tells us we should. He simply asks us to choose to be His. To sit in His lap, to stay close to Him, and to know He cares for us. He fights for us, defends us, protects us, and casts out fear.

There is a real battle for our heart and mind. The enemy's objective is to keep us from enjoying the peaceful presence of the Lord. Satan's goal is to render us useless through his deceptions. Believing his lies will thrust us into the bondage of fear and disable us from living a fulfilled life in our Father's kingdom.

"Fear not, for I am with you;
Be not dismayed, for I am your God.
I will strengthen you, Yes, I will help you,
I will uphold you with my righteous right hand."
Isaiah 41:10

"For God has not given us a spirit of fear,
but of power and of love and of a sound mind."
2 Timothy 1:7

JOY COMES IN THE MORNING
God delivers

I was in a difficult situation. I sought the Lord for answers through prayer and Bible study for several days and sleepless nights. I needed to know what God wanted me to do.

A longtime friend asked if her 18-year-old son could live with me in Oregon. She told me she wanted to help him find his way in the world, and she thought he could find a life in Oregon. She suggested he would be as helpful to me as I would be to him. I welcomed her suggestion and soon after he moved into my guestroom.

At first, he was pleasant. We went on a few outings, watched movies together, ate out, joked and laughed. He was considerate towards others and quickly became well known around town as a gentleman. Together we helped a friend on her farm where he eventually became employed. Someone even called him a godsend.

Gradually he became more disrespectful and demeaning. He criticized my friends and neighbors. He made off-handed remarks about the people at my church. Then he put down my brother and his family. His changed behavior effected the lives of a few young girls in town. To one he sent disturbing text messages. To another he disregarded her parent's restrictions about keeping his distance.

Finally, he turned his aggression towards me. He became argumentative and critical about insignificant things. He blatantly lied and fabricated stories that didn't happen, then argued as if they were real. He spoke about my possessions as though they were his. Finally, he asked inappropriate questions about the status of my will, wondering if his mom would inherit my home.

I finally confronted him about his behavior. I told him I never wanted to hear him say another unkind word about my family, friends or neighbors. I would never engage in another insignificant argument with him, and I wouldn't tolerate another lie or fabricated story as if it were true. As Christians, which he claimed to be one, I told him we have an obligation to be a positive influence in other people's lives. We are privileged to share the love of Christ with others who live among us. Being critical and lying is not of God. I emphasized that he was more important to me than engaging in unfruitful arguments that aren't based in a meaningful resolution. I reminded him that he invited himself to come live with me. If he was not willing to live in a Christ-pleasing way in my home, he was free to find another place to live.

In response, he went into a silent mode and didn't acknowledge anything I said. He left early in the morning for work and came home late without speaking to me. I became increasingly more uncomfortable in my own home.

The solution to this problem may seem obvious to most readers by now, but I needed to know exactly what God wanted me to do in this situation. The Holy Spirit led me to Psalm 101 where I had boldly written in the margin of my Bible, "LIVE LIKE THIS!" I remembered exactly when God lead me to this Psalm and why I wrote that comment in the margin. It was my promise to God in how I would honor Him for His generous gift in providing the home that I was now living in. In my New Living Translation Bible, Psalm 101 reads:

> "I will sing of your love and justice, Lord.
> I will praise you with songs.
> I will be careful to live a blameless life –
> when will you come to help me?
> I will lead a life of integrity in my own home.
> I will refuse to look at anything vile and vulgar.
> I hate all who deal crookedly;
> I will have nothing to do with them.
> I will reject perverse ideas and stay away from every evil.
> I will not tolerate people who slander their neighbors.
> I will not endure conceit and pride.
> I will search for faithful people to be my companions.
> Only those who are above reproach will be allowed to serve me.
> I will not allow deceivers to serve in my house,
> and liars will not stay in my presence.
> My daily task will be to ferret out the wicked
> and free the city of the Lord from their grip."

The following morning the Holy Spirit impressed upon me that I should tell this young man to move out of my house immediately, that very day. There was a deep sense of urgency. To allow him to postpone moving out would be disobedience on my part to what the Holy Spirit was saying.

The young man left for work before I woke up, so I telephoned him to say he needed to pack his things and move out. When he didn't answer his phone I left a voice message. He didn't reply to my call so later in the day I left him a text message.

I know this sounds harsh, it sounded harsh to me, but I couldn't escape the Holy Spirit's conviction. Each time I questioned this harsh action, God's reply was, "Do it NOW!" I heard this command all day.

At the end of the day the young men responded with a text that was a lie. He claimed he was still needed at work and wanted more time. I knew this wasn't true because I was in contact with his employer, my friend (the parent of the under-aged girl whom he refused to keep his distance). I later learned he lingered hoping to be invited to dinner. Instead he was encouraged to go.

When he arrived at my house I was thankful God made sure I wasn't alone to carry out this difficult task. A neighbor came to help keep the situation calm. He was one of my neighbors this young man criticized. Another neighbor across the street sat outside on his porch. They simply watched until his truck was packed and he drove away.

God immediately confirmed my actions were right. As soon as he left, my home was filled with a tangible sense of serenity I had never felt before. An obvious oppression had left and was replaced by an ever-present peace. Describing the obvious peace that flooded my home, a friend from church replied, "Of course, he took his evil minions with him. When he left, they left also."

 But that's not the end of the story.

That night I slept well but it wasn't a complete night's sleep. I had set my alarm for 3am to see the blood moon. I had never seen one and I didn't want to miss it. I sat outside in the crisp clear darkness and marveled at God's creation. At 4am I went back to bed. I gave myself permission to sleep in. I needed to catch up from the loss of sleep of the previous two nights, even though I had work to do.

My sleep was interrupted at 7am. My cell phone woke me with a whistle indicating I had a text message from my son. He owns a music studio and had sent me a song he just finished editing that he thought I would like. The song was titled "Joy." I was moved into tears. I just kicked out a friend's son the night before, one who created chaos and strife. On the following morning, my own son was blessing me with his beautiful God-given talent. Through him, God literally demonstrated that His "*joy comes in the morning.*" (Psalm 30:5). It felt like God couldn't wait to release His joy. It was if He was saying to Himself, "Do it NOW!" the very words He had urged me with the day before.

But that's still not the end of the story.

I was asked to share a part of this story with my church, of how God literally sent joy in the morning in the form of a song. I was left with a very short story excluding the events that preceded the blessing. While organizing my thoughts of what to say on Saturday evening, I felt the Holy Spirit tell me to wait for more of the story. That didn't make sense until my son called an hour later. After I told him I was sharing this story at church the next morning, he replied, "There's more to this story, want to hear it?"

He told me about the time he was on a road trip with a friend. He used the last of his money to put gas in the car that would take them home. It was all the money he had. While pulling the money out of his pocket he prayed, "God, this is all the money I have. I have no other money and I have no work lined up. I'm trusting you to provide for me." Just then his phone rang. It was the singer-songwriter asking him to record her song titled, "Joy."

Looking back, it's amazing to see the events that God created prior to the one that so deeply blessed me. I don't know the details that led to the writing of this song, or why my son was chosen to record it. But this I do know: God reached down and blessed those involved in this story at the exact moment each one needed to hear from Him, and He began planning it well in advance.

"For I know the plans I have for you," says the LORD.
"They are plans for good and not for disaster,
to give you a future and a hope."
Jeremiah 29:11 (NLT)

I GOT THEM

A vision of God's love and protection

I was woken by a horrible dream. It was 12:45am on July 10th, 2015. In my dream, my oldest daughter broke her ankle and I was taking her to the ER. A man helped carry her inside for a short distance then he insisted she walk on it. His suggestion was appalling. Her ankle started to fold into a narrow crease and was dangling loosely after each step. Even though I protested against his thoughtlessness and lack of caring, she continued to walk on it until it fell off. It was at this point that I woke up in a sweat, my heart pounding.

Now wide awake I began to pray, "Lord, please protect her and all my children."

It was then God gave me a vision. God doesn't usually give me visions, so when I received a clear picture in my mind it initially startled me. In the vision, I was looking down on all three of my children from an aerial view. I only saw the top of their heads. They were standing together with Jesus. Jesus was facing them wearing white. His arms were wrapped around them and He held them tightly against His chest. His head was bent down over theirs. The back of His white garment was stained red with blood from shielding the enemy's arrows that were meant for my children. The arrows were labeled lies, despair, destruction, hurt, and blame. In place of the arrows, Jesus was giving them truth, hope, shelter, protection, and comfort. With that image, Jesus spoke to my heart and mind. He said, "I got them. I got them."

His words instantly relieved me of my worry and gave me confidence they were in His care. I continue to be comforted to this day knowing Jesus is protecting them.

It's hard being a mom now that my children are grown. My love and concern for them has never diminished, nor will it. I know God's love for them is so much greater than my love, and His ability to care for them far exceeds mine. I now need to trust Him more with those I love the most. By revealing His great love and care for them He is revealing His deep love for me. In response, His love causes me to love Him even more.

"The eternal God is your refuge,
And underneath are the everlasting arms;
He will thrust out the enemy from before you,
And will say, 'Destroy!'"
Deuteronomy 33:27

REVEALED IN SAND
God's precious thoughts

God's precious thoughts of each of us are more in number than the grains of sand. Not only is that an incredible amount of thoughts, but what He's thinking about each of us is precious. No one can fathom the numbers of grains of sand on the entire earth, not to mention on one beach alone. I'm unable to count the number of grains in a small cup. Yet, this is how the Bible describes God's thoughts of us.

Sitting on the beach looking at the sand stretched to the horizon in both directions reminded me of this verse. It's one of my favorites.

"How precious also are Your thoughts to me, O God!
How great is the sum of them! If I should count them,
they would be more in number than the sand;"
Psalm 139:17-18a

I was at a women's retreat at the coast. I was sitting on the beach trying to think of a creative way to illustrate this verse to bless the women in my church. My first thought was to carry a cup of sand back to the meeting room. I envisioned a driftwood cross standing in it with this scripture attached. I abandoned this idea when spilled sand came to mind, which would turn a blessing into a burden. While thinking of another idea, I tied driftwood together with sea grass to form a small cross.

Then the idea came to mind to simply take a photo of the cross standing in the sand and later superimpose the verse over the photo. I walked down to the water's edge and placed the cross in the wet sand. I moved my camera around until a low perspective created an interesting composition. As I took the photo a young woman stepped into the picture. Her presence was perfect. When she approached me, I thanked her for being the perfect model and showed her the photo.

She asked what I was doing. I told her I was taking a photo to illustrate a Bible verse that says, "God's thoughts towards us are precious and more in number then the grains of sand."

"Wow!" she said. "That's cool, and this looks like a perfect place for prayers."

I hoped this verse encouraged her. I pray that each time she walks on the beach she will remember the vast number of God's precious thoughts of her. But as I thought more about the outcome, I came to realize I had little to do with it. My initial thoughts felt like my own until the sum of them revealed they were God's thoughts from the beginning, guiding my actions. He orchestrated the whole thing. I was only the vessel He used to tell a young woman His thoughts towards her are precious and innumerable.

TREE TRIMMING
God takes care of us

This might seem like a bit of a stretch to call this a God story. There was no supernatural event, or vision, or prophetic word. Everyone involved was simply doing what each one normally does. My mimosa tree needed to be trimmed and my neighbor was collecting wood for his daughter's wood burning stove.

My neighbor came with his son-in-law to trim the tree. When I asked him for his fee, he only asked me for $30. This small amount compared to the size of my tree made me uncomfortable. I didn't want to take advantage of my neighbor's generosity and hard work. When I asked God how much He wanted me to give my neighbor, I felt God impress upon me to give him $100, and not let him refuse it. That was the exact amount I received for extra work I did a few days before, and I saw it as God's provision for this purpose. I watched the two men work in the drizzling rain for most of the morning. They climbed up ladders and limbs to cut off long branches with a chainsaw. In the afternoon my neighbor's friend, a third man, also came to help.

When the three men finished trimming the tree I handed my neighbor the money in an envelope, that way he wouldn't see the amount and refuse it. However, when he returned with his trailer to haul off the wood, he told me I didn't need to give him that much. He said he only wanted $30, and that was for his son-in-law who needed the money and offered to work for it. My neighbor tried to return the extra money, but I told him the amount I gave was what God told me to give him. To not give him that amount would be disobedient to what God told me to do.

"OK," he said, "But that's an interesting amount. The additional money is the exact amount the third guy asked to borrow to help pay his rent." He asked if he could give the rest of the money to his friend for his help, that way it wouldn't need to be a loan. I agreed, seeing how God used four ordinary people and an overgrown mimosa tree to demonstrate how He provided for each person's needs.

My neighbor gained nothing for himself, or so it seemed. His daughter received the wood. Two helpers split the money. I benefited by having my tree trimmed. Payment for the job was provided for in advance.

That following Sunday during a Bible study at church, the question was asked, "Where have you seen Christ this last week?" That was easy for me to answer. I saw Jesus in my neighbor.

"And this same God who takes care of me
will supply all your needs from His glorious riches,
which have been given to us in Christ Jesus."
Philippians 4:19 (NLT)

WRITE ON
God rules

After God woke me on my fifty-fifth birthday instructing me to share these stories, He made it evident more than once afterwards that I should do so. One such event occurred early on.

Initially I handwrote each story in a journal. The constant editing by hand soon became tiring. I had a laptop, but months earlier it froze up from an invasive virus that made it irreparable. My office computer seemed like an obvious option, but it was uncomfortable to sit at for long periods of time.

To make the writing easier, I began searching online for a new laptop. By the end of the night I chose one to purchase. However, just before pressing the "Add to Cart" button, I felt the Lord prodding me to wait until morning and first try to restart my old one. It was so late at night my order probably wouldn't be processed until morning anyway, so I waited.

In the morning, I felt the Lord say to my spirit, "If I can heal people, I can repair a laptop." I was curious to know if He would actually do it. I dug my old laptop out of the closet and plugged it in to charge the battery. I didn't expect much, the virus made it impossible to access any part of it. The home screen was replaced with an official-looking page containing large titles, gold emblems, and a demanded of $200 to unlock my computer. Within the page was a window using my laptop's camera viewer to record me looking at my computer screen. It startled me.

I have no logical explanation for what happened next. When I turned my laptop on, the normal home screen appeared prompting me for my password. Because it had been so long since I entered the password I couldn't remember it. I sat there a moment just staring at it, wondering how to create a new password. Then it came to me, and I'm going to tell it to you because it's relevant to this story. It was: "GodRules." After I typed in the password it logged in normally. I cautiously maneuvered through the various pages without a glitch. I typed on it for the rest of the day.

That night I went to Bible study anxious to tell my friends that God fixed my laptop. A friend and I arrived at the front door at the same time, but the door was locked, which was unusual. I couldn't remember it being locked before. When our friend inside came to unlock the door, she first opened it just a crack. She peered around it in a joking manner and smiled. I asked if we needed a password to enter.

"Yes," she said. "It's: God Rules."

"What! How did you know?" I asked.

"Know what?" she wondered.

After I told her this story, she said she had no idea why she chose that password. She had never thought of it before.

I continued using the laptop to write all these stories. I asked my cousin, an IT Tech, if he knew of computers being cleared of a virus on their own. He said he hadn't.

God used that old laptop on several occasions to prod me to continue writing these stories. When I had time to write, but choosing to do other things instead, the laptop's motor would cycle on all by itself even though it had been off for several days. It was like God was saying, "What are you doing? Get to it!"

"The LORD has established His throne in heaven,
And His kingdom rules over all."
(even a virus-infected laptop)
Psalm 103:19

CALLED OUT
God's plans supersede our plans

My friend in the last story who unlocked the door and suggested the password, "God Rules," told me about a miraculous healing of her friend's son after a man prayed for him. The man himself was miraculously healed after being crushed by a logging truck. Learning this man would be speaking at a church in Portland, several of us went to hear his inspirational testimony. It was November of 2015.

I was told of this man's willingness to pray over all who attend his meetings. I anticipated witnessing God do amazing things through those who received prayer. However, I decided in advance to not ask for prayer. I felt I was in a good relationship with God and didn't need a man to pray for me. Instead, I planned to watch God bless others.

While listening to the speaker's testimony I was distracted several times by something tapping on the outside of my right calf. I thought my friend sitting next to me was playfully poking my leg, but she was too far away to reach me without being noticed. It was a definite repeated tapping, but every time I looked down I saw nothing touching me. I became disturbed to the point that I thought something was seriously wrong with my leg.

After the speaker shared his moving testimony it was obvious the Holy Spirit was moving in that place. Many gathered to share words of encouragement and wisdom. Those seeking prayer formed a long line in front. I walked to the book table in the back of the room.

After praying for half the people, the speaker stopped to called out to the audience. He asked, "Does anyone here know a Shane? Someone you have been praying for, but your prayers have gone unanswered?" At that moment, I felt a single heavy tap on my heart, like the previous tapping on my leg, only harder. This led me to wonder if the leg-tapping was from God to get my attention.

My nephew's name is Shane. He's my brother's son, and I was praying for him. Even though I was emotionally moved by this interruption, I dismissed it. I wasn't planning to go forward for prayer, so I imagined someone else there knew a Shane whom they were praying for.

My friends lingered at church reuniting with others. I mostly watched to see if someone else said they were praying for a Shane. No one did. When the line shortened we were encouraged to go forward for prayer. I agreed, but only to ask if he said Shane, as someone in the back of the room thought he said Shania. If he said Shane, I wanted to know if someone already went forward.

I was third from the last in line, with one friend in front of me and two other friends behind me. I was trying to be last in line, but I couldn't persuade my polite friends to go ahead of me. As my friend in front of me went forward for prayer, I stood at a distance waiting my turn. When the speaker finished praying for my friend, she only took a few steps away and watched me walk forward. I asked the speaker if he called out the name Shane or Shania, because my nephew's name is Shane.

Enthusiastically he proclaimed, "You're the one!"

God's loving presence instantly overwhelmed me and I was moved to tears unable to say another word. The speaker prayed for Shane's salvation, but it was the end of his prayer that affected me personally. I felt as if God was speaking directly to me as he prayed. He said, "God is your Father and you are His daughter, and He has heard your prayers."

Though I predetermined to not receive prayer, God made sure I did. He knew I needed mending from deep within. For when I heard these words prayed, I literally felt my broken heart healed from all its past wounds.

After he prayed I turned to look at my friend standing in front of me. Wiping her face, she said, "As soon as he said, 'You're the one,' I burst into tears."

This experience brought me into a deeper relationship with God. Not only did He heal my heart, He also strengthened it. In addition to what God did for me, He increased the faith of my friends who were there. Likewise, my brother and sister-in-law, Shane's parents, marveled at the power of God on behalf of their son, and their faith was strengthened. The retelling of this story later increased the faith of a neighbor who believe God can heal more than physical ailments. That new faith led to prayer for a broken relationship that was later mended. My own prayers have increased in boldness because now I know, I mean I really, really know, that God is my Father and I am His daughter.

For those with unseen injuries, deep within, only God is able to heal that wound. And He wants to. In doing so, He will prove to you He is genuinely trustworthy. He will never hurt or betray you, not ever! His love for you is so great, so deep, and so vast. His whole being is love, and what God loves most is you!

He heals the brokenhearted
And binds up their wounds.
Psalm 147:3

CRACKED BASEMENT

God works through our imperfections

The sump pump's constant motoring throughout the night reminded me I still had water seepage in the basement. Winters in Oregon are wet; thus, the water table gets very high. Water can flow through the tiniest hairline cracks in a concrete floor.

In the morning, I put on my rubber boots and went downstairs to see what was happening. Two weeks prior I repaired the old seals that broke from the water pressure of the last big storm. The recent rain added to the already saturated ground forcing water to come up in new places. Shallow streams merged together as they flowed continuously toward the drain.

Frustrated I voiced my thoughts out loud, "God, what about all those days and nights I already spent patching the floor! I thought I had this fixed!"

His reply penetrated my heart and thoughts with, "I want you to be like your floor."

"What!? God, that doesn't make any sense. You want me to be something annoying that needs constant repair?"

God continued to speak to my heart with, "I want you to allow My Holy Spirit to flow through you and spill out into the lives of others." The boot prints where I walked through the shallow streams made it clear what God was teaching.

I started to cry because I knew it would require me to trust Him more. I also knew this meant I needed to be more vulnerable; admitting I'm flawed and imperfect and busted up in areas. I relented, agreeing to allow the Holy Spirit to seep through my cracks for His glory and for the benefit of others.

In the Bible, the Holy Spirit is often depicted as water. Water penetrates and seeps through the smallest of cracks and holes. Once it begins flowing it is hard to contain, as I was learning from my basement. When the water is stopped in one area, it continues to flow until it finds another location to seep through.

Dear reader, please know I am praying for you. May the living water of the Holy Spirit seep into your cracks to bless you. Then may the work He does in your heart generously flow through you to bless others.

"For I will pour water on him who is thirsty,
and floods on the dry ground;
I will pour My Spirit on your descendants,
and My blessing on your offspring;"
Isaiah 44:3

"On the last day, that great day of the feast, Jesus stood and cried out,
saying, 'If anyone thirsts, let him come to Me and drink.
He who believes in Me, as the scripture has said, out of his heart
will flow rivers of living water.'" But this He spoke concerning the Spirit,
whom those believing in Him would receive;"
John 7:37-39

DAILY BREAD

God orchestrates events and circumstances

I left the hair salon Saturday morning and walked next door to the coffee shop. An older woman standing outside on the sidewalk asked me where the bakery was. I told her I hadn't seen one in that shopping center but would like to also know where it was.

She said, "I bet someone inside knows where it is."

I followed her into the coffee shop. She approached the first man she saw standing between the door and the counter. He was conversing with the barista.

"Excuse me, do you know where the bakery is?"

"Yes," he said, "I'm the baker, and I just delivered some freshly baked bread that is available for sale here."

"O wonderful! Did you bring any baguettes?"

"Yes," he replied, "I just took them out of the oven. They're still warm."

Tickled by this interaction I expressed my thoughts to those inside. I said this seemed like more than mere coincidence. The woman standing outside *knew* someone inside would know

139

where the bakery was. The first person she saw was the baker, the most likely person to know of the bakery. Furthermore, the baguettes she was seeking were there, fresh out of the oven, and available.

I asked the woman her name. She said, "Victoria."

"Wow, that's coincidental," replied the barista. "My name is Vicky."

Again, another coincidence that told me God was in the details. Jesus tells us in Matthew 4:4,

"It is written, man shall not live by bread alone,
but by every word that proceeds from the mouth of God."

It's true, we have the need to eat, but it's not only physical bread we crave. We also have a deep desire to know God and to know that our Creator knows us. He will gladly reveal Himself to us when we look for Him. The more we see Him, the easier it becomes to recognize Him when He does appear. His divine appointments are typically little events like this where He simply pops into a moment of our day to say, "Here I AM."

This particular morning God wasn't speaking in an audible voice. He was revealing His ability to orchestrate events. He provided bread for the woman, income for the baker and the coffee shop, a delightful coincidence for the barista, and a story for me to share that He did it.

"And Jesus said to them, "I am the bread of life.
He who comes to Me shall never hunger,
and he who believes in Me shall never thirst."
John 6:35

PLANETS ON PARADE
God revealed in creation

God reveals Himself through events each person enjoys. It may not be a significant occasion, but one that is recognizable to the person experiencing it. Perhaps you can remember a moment in your life when God revealed Himself to you through something you enjoy. This is one such moment that God revealed Himself to me personally, simply letting me know He was near and in control.

It's no surprise I enjoy the heavenly realm above us. This is my third story about activity in the night sky. But this story is about more than what God does in the heavens. Just as He creates and orchestrates creation around us, He also creates every event and circumstance in our personal lives.

It was October 9, 2015 and I was up early while it was still dark outside. Over the café curtains in my kitchen I saw three very large bright stars next to the moon. I threw on my warm coat and went outside for a clearer view. A quick online search revealed they were Venus, Mars, and Jupiter lining up with the waning crescent moon. Mercury was coming up over the horizon and Saturn was a tiny speck off in the distance. It was being called, "Planets on Parade."

I sat on my front steps in the dark mesmerized by their alignment. But like a parade that goes down the street I felt a bit awkward sitting there by myself, having no one to "ooh" and "ahh" with. Thinking others might enjoy the Parade I posted a quick note on social media then sent a text to my brother who is usually up before dawn.

When the rising sun brightened the sky, and the parading planets vanished from view, I went back inside to begin my day. I didn't hear back from my brother and there was no response on my social media post. I hoped others saw it but at the time I was a bit disappointed watching it alone.

Later that morning I received a text with a photo from my brother that read, "How it looked from my house." He saw it thirty minutes before I texted him while driving to work. Next my aunt sent a text. She saw the moon and planets long before she saw my online post.

I understand this may not be significant to anyone else, but to me it was. When I lived in California, clear skies were the norm. I often watched stars pass through the night sky and had other family members to share these events with. I am now living in Oregon where cloud cover in October is the norm. Don't get me wrong; I love clouds. But when an event happens in the night sky, and there are no clouds hiding it from view, I get excited. I marveled at God's handiwork, not only for creating a spectacular sight in the heavens, but also for clearing the cloud cover for my enjoyment. Then He revealed I wasn't watching His parading planets alone, but with two close relatives.

When little events happen that delight you, don't take them lightly. Consider the Creator's hand at work in the moments that He may have created simply to delight you. He wants you to know He cares about the things you care about, because what He ultimately cares about most is you.

"For since the creation of the world His invisible attributes are
clearly seen, being understood by the things that are made,
even His eternal power and Godhead,
so that they are without excuse,"
Romans 1:20

SIDEWALK SUNDAY SCHOOL
God instructs and teaches

I felt as though I shouldn't go to Sunday school. Something about that morning made me feel hindered and held back. There was an inner nagging that said, "Don't rush off."

Even my cat was acting unusually agitated. He passed in front of me and got in my way. He blocked the door, and demanded I give him extra attention. I said to him, "You're acting like Balaam's donkey, just speak to me."

The Sunday school lesson at my church was teaching how Jesus' life has impacted society throughout the world. For the first two classes I gave an elderly friend a ride. For this third class, she called to say she felt ill and was staying home. I was sorry she was sick, but her call solved the dilemma of telling her I wouldn't be able to give her a ride to church if God was preventing me from going.

I never felt hindered from attending church before. I assumed this was an enemy distraction. Uncertain of God's instruction, I slowly walked to my car as if to leave. I was hoping for a clear sign from God that He didn't want me to go. Forgetting something in the house, I went back inside. When I returned to my car I saw my neighbor's sister waving to me from across the street. I felt the Lord instruct me to talk with her and to take my time.

I walked across the street to say hello as she stepped off the porch to meet me on the sidewalk. She told me how she was learning to trust God more. We talked about how God is the only true God who is trustworthy. I told her God's thoughts towards us are precious and more in number than the grains of sand.

"Wow," she said. "I never knew that."

Shortly after, another neighbor down the street walked over from her house to join us. This was unusual; I rarely saw anyone outside on Sunday morning. It was becoming obvious God was orchestrating something.

My neighbor across the street, who planned to meet me at church later, came out of her house to ask, "What? You're not going to Sunday school?"

"No." I said, "I have a weird feeling the Lord is hindering me from going."

"Well," she asked, "Can I ride with you to church later so my husband can use the truck? He wants to use it to get gas for the lawn mower."

Just then her husband came out from around the side of the house to where we four women are talking. He asked, "So, what are you gals doin'?"

I told him, "I'm stalling going to church because God heard your prayer of needing the truck."

"Yeah," He said to his wife, "God heard my prayer!"

We all laughed and agreed that God knows in advance what we need, and then provides for that need. It was obvious God was impacting our little corner of the world with a sweet morning gathering of neighbors.

"I will instruct you and teach you
in the way you should go;
I will guide you with My eye."
Psalm 32:8

FATHER'S BUSINESS
Meeting other believers

In a large store, a man called out to me from his empty checkout line. He said, "It's had been a crazy busy day until now." I was happy his register was open.

I'm not sure exactly how we landed on the topic of God. It must have been the Holy Spirit's leading. He told me he was a preacher. While earning extra income, he was doing what he could to spread the good news at that store.

After I made my purchase there was no one in line after me. We continued to share God stories, agreeing our meeting was a divine appointment. He said the staff calls him the store minister. When sharing his faith with others, he tells them, "I have to be about my Father's business."

The checker behind him turned around to join our conversation. There wasn't anyone in her line either. I smiled and told her we were having church. She frowned.

"Ah," he said, "Today is her last day, she's a bit sad."

I told her God may be calling her to be a missionary elsewhere. The store minister said he already told her the same thing. It was obvious she was going to miss his fellowship. It was also apparent God had arraigned this timely meeting that reminded us to always be involved in doing the Father's business.

"And whatever you do, do it heartily, as to the Lord
and not to men, knowing that from the Lord you will receive
the reward of the inheritance; for you serve the Lord Christ."
Colossians 3:23-24

WIND

God speaks to us through His creation

It was 2am. God woke me with the impression I was to go outside to pray. I knew this thought was from God because I wouldn't naturally think of it, especially in January. It was 27 degrees outside. My thought was to stay inside under my warm blankets. Yet, because I was wide awake, thinking a thought I would never have imagined on my own, I felt this was the leading of the Holy Spirit. I was curious to know why.

I climbed out of bed, put on my slippers, a big jacket and a scarf. I expected to see something awesome in the night sky similar to constellations God revealed to me in the past. Instead, the sky was dark gray from clouds with a faint glow in the distance that I assumed was the moon.

Knowing God wanted me to pray, I sat on the porch steps and asked God to protect my children from harm, shield them from deception, and keep them free from oppression. I asked God to increase their faith, to give them clarity of mind, to give them wisdom and knowledge of His truth. I asked Him to reveal His deep love and mighty power. I asked Him to give them favor with others towards the things that bring them joy, and to lead them on the path towards a fruitful life. As always, I asked God to show up in their day to reveal Himself to them in a tangible way.

As I made each request the wind increased, blowing towards me from the south. Strong gusts rustled loudly through the distant fir trees. Yet, where I sat the air was still. It was an interesting sensation hearing the forceful wind without feeling it.

Thirty minutes later I went back to bed, but I never went back to sleep. I wondered why God called me outside to pray. There were only clouds and wind. To be honest, I was a little disappointed until later that morning. The next chapter marked in my Bible to read was Psalm 104. Speaking of God, verses 3-4a (NLT) reads,

"You lay out the rafters of Your home in the rain clouds.
You make the clouds Your chariot;
You ride upon the wings of the wind.
The winds are Your messengers;"

Then I understood why God guided me outside to pray. The experience made me feel close to Him. Or rather, it felt like He came close to me. My Maker invited me to sit outside with Him to reveal He was metaphorically overhead riding on His clouds. The winds were used to make His presence known and tell me He was near to hear my prayers.

Even though I couldn't feel the wind, the effects of the wind were evident the next morning. Tree limbs had fallen, brush was scattered, and items left in the yard moved from their previous location. People in town were discussing the wind's fierceness, yet I had only heard it momentarily while sitting outside in the dark between 2-2:30am.

BIG TIP

God is faithful

Have you ever experienced God leading you to pray for something that you knew He could accomplish, yet wondered if He really would? I know God can answer prayer, especially those He initiates. What I lacked was the faith to reveal the prayer to the person I was praying for. I didn't want them to be disappointed if God didn't answer it. Yet that is exactly what God asked me to do.

The need for prayer began just before noon. My daughter sent me a text message to say she was feeling really sad. She was at work, so we couldn't talk on the phone. While I prayed for her, I felt God wanted me to write the prayer. As I did He began to reveal His heart for her.

Jan 9 2017 @ 12 noon
as the bells in Town are ringing

Praying for Kristin:
Oh God, Powerful + Mighty! Full of love +
compassion for all Your creation, especially Your people.
Today, send Your people to Kristin To speak blessings
into her life. If people won't go, send angels.
If angels can't go, Jesus I ask if you will go + wrap
Your loving arms around her, fill her with Your joy,
and love, and the light of Your truth that she is
greatly loved + cherished. BIND all evil oppression,
Cast it far from her, renew her mind, heart + soul
with Your great power. I know You can do it !!!
I know You love her.
    And one more thing: Cause someone
to tip her 100⁰⁰, to just hand it to her personally,
if not a person, Then an angel. If not an angel, Then
You Jesus. Prove to her You love + care for
every thing about her. Cause her to feel your
presence. Do this for her because I believe
YOU can do iT! Amen

When I finished praying, I believed God told me to text a photo of my hand-written prayer to my daughter. I hesitated at first mainly because of the part about the $100 tip. Where she worked tips were divided. I had no doubt God would comfort her, but I wasn't sure about the tip. It was so specific. I imagined someone secretly handing her a $100 bill. But, why would they? It seemed so extravagant. Nervously I sent her the photo.

That evening she called to say someone she knew came to the café and noticed she seemed sad. Outside, at one of the tables, he prayed for her. He later returned to see how she was doing. She told me his prayers made a difference and she felt much better. She didn't say anything about a big tip.

A week later she called with some exciting news. The café cleaned out a miscellaneous drawer that contained odds-and-ends and lost-and-found items. In the back of the drawer someone found two BART (Bay Area Rapid Transit) cards. They are prepaid cards for riding the train system in the San Francisco Bay Area. They were held for customers who left them behind several months prior.

As they were never claimed, they were given to my daughter. She was the only one working at the café who rode the BART train to get to work. No one thought there was any amount on them since they weren't claimed. However, on her way home she checked the amount on the cards at the BART Station. One contained $40, the other contained $80. It was slightly more than $100, and she didn't have to share them with anyone else.

"He who calls you is faithful, who also will do it."
1 Thessalonians 5:24

FLAT TIRE

God uses others to warn us

I was leaving my CPA's office. I backed my car out of its parking space beside a three-foot high hedge that grew between the parking lot and the sidewalk. At the edge of the tiny driveway I waited for a car on my left to pass. The driver slowed down then parked in front of me, blocking my way out. Even though I knew the driver couldn't hear me, I threw my hands up and said, "You can't park there!"

A woman got out and pointed to my car. She was shouting something I couldn't hear. When I got out of my car she shouted again, "You have a flat tire! Your tire is flat! Go to Les Schwab NOW!" Then she drove away. You may be thinking, so what, a woman warned you about your flat tire. Where's the evidence of God in this story?

There is no logical way she could have seen my right front tire behind a hedge, approaching from my left side. She either had X-ray vision, was an angel, or the Holy Spirit instructed her to do so. Either way, I was thankful.

The fact that she told me exactly where to go was also helpful. For when she told me I had a flat all I could think of was the extra expense to buy a new tire after I paid my CPA a hefty fee for preparing my taxes. It was the extra help I needed to snap me out of my shock. Les Schwab was only two blocks away.

Once at the tire shop, I looked at my tire again, but it only looked low. The tire tech assured me it was flat. I followed him inside as he told the sales girl to write me up for a flat tire. I anticipated spending more money that day and I wasn't happy. From where I waited I could see the rear end of my car parked half way out the service bay. There were several people ahead of me so I knew I'd be there a while. I started doodling in my sketchbook to pass the time. Each time a tire tech came through the door I expected a quote for the new tire. When all previous customers were gone, my car was still halfway in the service bay, so I continued to draw.

"Are you Kim?" The sales girl called out to me from across the room.

"Yes," I said, expecting a bill.

"Is that your car parked outside?" pointing to my car which had been moved in front of the glass entry doors. I asked if I needed to pay for a new front tire.

"No, you just had a screw in it and we pulled it out. You're free to go."

I was so relieved. Her statement made me think of Jesus' words in John 8:36,

"Therefore, if the Son makes you free, you shall be free indeed."

I will never comprehend how the woman knew my tire was flat. I am very grateful for her warning, for she was a godsend.

"For as many as are led by the Spirit of God,
these are sons of God."
Romans 8:14

The following story has been added simply to illustrate that I'm an ordinary person. In fact, I often feel like the silliest dork in a group. Yet, in spite of all my shortcomings, God is willing to have a relationship with me, proving He is willing to have a relationship with everyone. I vowed to never let this story be public, but I also never imagined God would instruct me to publish His stories in a book. I hope this story reveals that no one needs to be perfect to have a relationship with God, only willing. Everything that is perfect is of Him; that's His department.

PAPER
God's servants are brave

I was flying to Minnesota for a family reunion. The night before the flight I set my alarm for 5:30 but forgot to specify A.M. The alarm didn't go off in the morning. Waking up late I quickly dressed, grabbed my bag, and raced to the airport praying all the way. In Oregon, police give tickets for exceeding the speed limit by 5mph.

I made it to the gate just as a flight attendant at the counter picked up the microphone. Instead of giving boarding instructions, he announced our pilot was sick. There would be an hour delay while we waited for another pilot. For those with quick connecting flights, this was bad news. For me, this was great news! I now had time to go to the bathroom, get a cup of coffee and something to eat. I even had time to walk around a little.

I returned to the gate a little early and stood near the front of the line. My seat was in the back of the plane and this airline called last rows first, so I waited my turn to board.

Standing next to me was a tall man, a stunning American Indian impeccably dressed. His leather cowboy hat, over his long dark braids, was decorated with a silver and turquoise band. His cinnamon colored long-sleeved T-Shirt was neatly tucked into his cinnamon colored jeans. His leather belt matched his hat that matched his boots. He looked like he was going to a special event.

After a few moments, he leaned over towards me and pointed to my back pocket. With a deep voice in a slow rhythm he uttered one word, "Pa-per" (like a child might mimic an Indian saying, "Howw").

I thought my boarding pass was falling out of my back pocket, but I found it empty. I looked at him and shrugged my shoulders to let him know I didn't understand.

He pointed to my back again and repeated, "Pa-per."

I checked my pockets again, still found nothing, and shrugged at him as before.

Then he slowly leaned towards me, reached into the waistband of my jeans, pulled out a toilet seat cover and handed it to me. Being in the front of the line magnified my embarrassment. I also wondered how many people noticed me walk out of the restroom, stand in line for coffee, or stroll around the airport. No one said a word to me except this man. After my humiliation wore off, I came to realize he was a very brave Brave.

Waiting in the Denver airport for my connecting flight I had little to do but think about my "Pa-per" embarrassment. I texted this story to my sister-in-law, then asked what her most embarrassing moment was. Her return text read, "It doesn't matter, you win."

Finally arriving at the Sioux Falls airport, I was greeted by my aunt and uncle. Naturally, they asked how my flight was. I told them my embarrassing "Pa-per" story. I didn't think to ask them to not share this humiliating story with anyone else. Their closest neighbor lived a mile away and later that week we'd be busy at a threshing bee. However, if you're from the country, you know news mysteriously travels faster there. When we gathered for dinner at the bee a week later, someone I barely know leaned across the table to say, "I'd like to hear your story about the Pa-per."

"But God has chosen the foolish things
of the world to put to shame the wise,
and God has chosen the weak things
of the world to put to shame
the things which are mighty;
and the base things of the world
and the things which are despised
God has chosen,
and the things which are not,
to bring to nothing the things that are,
that no flesh should glory in His presence."
1 Corinthians 1:27-29

DEAR READER

In closing, if there is just one thing I can tell you, it's that:
GOD IS AWESOME!

Seriously! My heart feels like it wants to explode trying to express this truth to you. If you've never had an encounter with Him, all preconceived notions of Him are skewed. No imagination can comprehend His power, His ability to save, rescue, restore, or redeem. For if you have never experienced God personally you haven't experienced real joy, real excitement, real freedom.

I know, there are people and events in this world that are downright evil. I've encountered wicked people and I've been in evil situations. But just because they exist doesn't mean God can't prove to you His power over that evil. For that is exactly what Jesus did on the cross and continues to do to this day.

I hope this book pointed you to God and illustrated Him in a way you have never seen or thought of before. Hopefully my experiences with God created a desire in you to know Him more deeply and to trust Him more fully. Perhaps for the first time you will ask Him, "God if you are real, prove it to me." If you do, I already know He will answer you.

I've discovered that true joy and hope are only found in Jesus, where fear and anxiety diminish. Once you put your trust in the One who loves and cares for you beyond your comprehension, then you will discover He is truly trustworthy in every area of your life. How did I come to believe this? I have lived it. God persistently called me to Himself until I could no longer resist. Once I submitted I discovered a love so deep words can never express it. After I experienced His love I had a desire to know Him more, leading me to read about Him in the Bible. My study of His word brought me closer to Him. Its lessons encouraged me to trust, believe, and follow God like those in it. The Bible taught me to trust in the unseeable, fight without weapons, move without a plan, follow in faith, and speak with boldness. After reading of the miraculous works of the Holy Spirit, through Christ's followers in the book of Acts, I said to myself, "I want to live like that." Maybe you do, too.

All the stories in this book began with a study of the scriptures and applying them in any given situation. I wasn't trusting in the ink-printed words themselves, or the paper the text was written on, but I trusted in One the words spoke of. The source of true life and joy and meaning originates from God. The Bible is His written word. In it you'll find His love, guidance, protection, shelter, provision, or whatever you need.

When you begin to seriously study the Bible, and believe what it says, you're going to encounter God. As you seek Him, He's going to reveal Himself to you. As a result, you're going to have your own God stories. Your God stories will encourage others in their faith, substantiate the existence of God, and demonstrate His desire to have a relationship with us. They are His stories, and they are meant to be shared.

"Many, O LORD my God,
are Your wonderful works which You have done;
And Your thoughts toward us cannot be recounted to You in order;
if I would declare and speak of them,
they are more than can be numbered."
Psalm 40:5

Since knowing Jesus, my main desire has been to point others to Him. I don't have the answers to each person's circumstances, but He does. The Bible tells us Jesus has authority over everything. If that's true, and I personally believe it is, then He is the one we need to follow, learn from, and trust. In Luke 21:26-28, Jesus tells us,

"And there will be signs in the sun, in the moon, and in the stars; and on the earth distress of nations, with perplexity, the sea and the waves roaring; men's hearts failing them from fear and expectation of those things which are coming on the earth, for the powers of the heavens will be shaken. Then they will see the Son of Man coming in a cloud with power and great glory. Now when these things begin to happen, look up and lift up your heads, because your redemption draws near."

Salvation is only found in JESUS.

STORIES BY TOPIC

Answered Prayer

Angels

Boldness to Speak Out

Creation

Divine Appointments

God's Guidance

Healing

Humility

Humor

Instruction

Joy of the Lord

Leading of the Holy Spirit

Obedience

Protection

Provision

Salvation

Small Miracles

Struggles

Visions

Witnessing

ABOUT THE AUTHOR

Kimberly Shaw is a self-employed artist, designer, and owner of Kimberly Shaw Graphics where she has been in the business of making people smile since 1994. Her tea-themed stationery is sold nationwide in tea rooms, gift stores, boutiques, stationery stores, antique stores, historical museums, flower shops, and garden centers. Find Kimberly's products and information on her website at kimberlyshawgraphics.com.

"Meant To Be Shared" is available in Book and Kindle format at Amazon.com and on her website at kimberlyshawgraphics.com.

Follow Kimberly's journey of faith and creativity on her blog, "Greetings" at kimberlyshaw.typepad.com and on:

www.facebook.com/KimberlyShawGraphics

www.instagram.com/kimberlyshawgraphics

www.instagram.com/meanttobeshared_thebook

www.pinterest.com/kimberlyshawgraphics

Made in the
USA
Lexington, KY